First World War
and Army of Occupation
War Diary
France, Belgium and Germany

16 DIVISION
Divisional Troops
156 Field Company Royal Engineers
29 July 1915 - 31 May 1919

WO95/1965/2

The Naval & Military Press Ltd
www.nmarchive.com
Published in association with The National Archives

Published by

The Naval & Military Press Ltd

Unit 10 Ridgewood Industrial Park,

Uckfield, East Sussex,

TN22 5QE England

Tel: +44 (0) 1825 749494

www.naval-military-press.com

www.nmarchive.com

This diary has been reprinted in facsimile from the original. Any imperfections are inevitably reproduced and the quality may fall short of modern type and cartographic standards.

© Crown Copyright
Images reproduced by permission of The National Archives, London, England, 2015.

Contents

Document type	Place/Title	Date From	Date To
Heading	WO95/1965. 16 Division Headquarters Branches & Service Dec 1915-May 1919 156 Field Company Royal Engineers		
Heading	16th Division 156th Field Coy R.E. Dec 1915-May 1919		
Heading	156th F.C.R.E. 16th Div B.E.F. 19.12.15 Vol I		
War Diary	Dover	29/07/1915	29/07/1915
War Diary	Chatham.	04/08/1915	19/08/1915
War Diary	Moore Park	18/08/1915	09/09/1915
War Diary	Blackdown	24/11/1915	31/11/1915
War Diary	Henley On Thames	01/11/1915	20/11/1915
War Diary	Blackdown	24/11/1915	30/11/1915
Heading	156 F. Co. R.E. Dec. Vol.		
War Diary	Blackdown	01/12/1915	18/12/1915
War Diary	Havre	19/12/1915	21/12/1915
War Diary	Noeux Les Mines	22/12/1915	31/12/1915
Heading	16th Div. 156th F.C.R.E. Vol. 2 Jan 16		
War Diary	Noeux Les Mines.	01/01/1916	31/01/1916
Heading	156 Field Coy RE Vol III		
War Diary	Noeux Les Mines	01/02/1916	15/02/1916
War Diary	Cuhem	16/02/1916	27/02/1916
War Diary	La Miquellerie	28/02/1916	28/02/1916
War Diary	Beuvry	29/02/1916	29/02/1916
Miscellaneous	DAAG (1)	04/04/1916	04/04/1916
Heading	156 F.C.R.E Vol 4		
War Diary	Beuvry	01/03/1916	02/03/1916
War Diary	Braquemont	03/03/1916	04/03/1916
War Diary	Les Brebis	05/03/1916	14/03/1916
War Diary	Lapugnoy	15/03/1916	23/03/1916
War Diary	Philosophe	24/03/1916	24/03/1916
War Diary	Lapugnoy	24/03/1916	25/03/1916
War Diary	Philosophe	25/03/1916	31/03/1916
Miscellaneous	DAAG (1)	05/05/1916	05/05/1916
War Diary	Philosophe	01/04/1916	31/05/1916
Heading	D.A.G. 3rd Echelon G.H.Q		
War Diary	Philosophe	01/06/1916	30/06/1916
Heading	War Diary 156th Field Coy Royal Engineers 1st. July to 31st. July 1916. Volume No. 8		
War Diary	Philosophe	01/07/1916	31/07/1916
Heading	War Diary. 156th Field Coy R.E. Month Of August, 1916. Volume 9		
War Diary	Philosophe	01/08/1916	25/08/1916
War Diary	Hurionville	26/08/1916	31/08/1916
Heading	War Diary 156th Field Company R.E. For Month Of September, 1916. Volume 10		
War Diary	Citadel	01/09/1916	04/09/1916
War Diary	Billon Farm	05/09/1916	06/09/1916
War Diary	Carnoy	07/09/1916	07/09/1916
War Diary	Guillemont	07/09/1916	10/09/1916
War Diary	Vaux	11/09/1916	17/09/1916

War Diary	Huppy	18/09/1916	21/09/1916
War Diary	Meteren	22/09/1916	24/09/1916
War Diary	Scherpenberg.	25/09/1916	30/09/1916
Heading	War Diary Month Of October, 1916. Volume 11 156th Field Co. R.E. Vol 11		
War Diary	Scherpenberg	01/10/1916	03/10/1916
War Diary	R.C. Farm.	04/10/1916	25/10/1916
War Diary	Pioneer Fm	26/10/1916	31/10/1916
Heading	War Diary. For Month Of November, 1916. Volume 12. 156th Field Coy. R.E.		
War Diary	Pioneer Fm.	01/11/1916	30/11/1916
Heading	War Diary For Month Of December, 1916. 156th Field Coy R.E. Vol 13		
War Diary	Pioneer Fm	01/12/1916	05/12/1916
War Diary	Lurgan Camp	06/12/1916	11/12/1916
War Diary	Dranoutre	12/12/1916	31/12/1916
Heading	War Diary for month of January, 1917. Volume 14 Royal Engineers 156th Field Company		
War Diary	Dranoutre	01/01/1917	31/01/1917
Heading	War Diary. For Month Of February, 1917. Volume 15 Unit:- 156th Field Coy R.E.		
War Diary	Dranoutre.	01/02/1917	28/02/1917
Heading	War Diary For Month of March, 1917. Volume 16 Unit:- 156th Field Company R.E.		
War Diary	Dranoutre	01/03/1917	17/03/1917
War Diary	Baldoyle Camp	18/03/1917	21/03/1917
War Diary	Fletre	22/03/1917	31/03/1917
Heading	War Diary For Month Of April, 1917. Volume 17 Unit:- 156th Field Coy R.E.		
War Diary	R.E. Fm. Kemmel	01/04/1917	30/04/1917
Heading	War Diary. Volume 18 For Month Of May, 1917. Unit 156th Field Coy Royal Eng		
War Diary	RE. Farm	01/05/1917	06/05/1917
War Diary	De Zon	07/05/1917	08/05/1917
War Diary	Baldoyle	09/05/1917	10/05/1917
War Diary	Wouldham Camp	11/05/1917	12/05/1917
War Diary	Upnor Camp	13/05/1917	23/05/1917
War Diary	Chatham Camp	24/05/1917	31/05/1917
Heading	War Diary. For Month Of June, 1917. Volume 19 Unit 156th Field Company R.E		
War Diary	Chatham Camp	01/06/1917	09/06/1917
War Diary	Chatham Camp Locre.	10/06/1917	12/06/1917
War Diary	Kemmel	13/06/1917	17/06/1917
War Diary	Outtersteene	18/06/1917	21/06/1917
War Diary	Poperinghe	22/06/1917	30/06/1917
Heading	War Diary. For Month Of July, 1917. Volume 20 Unit-156th Field Coy R.E.		
War Diary	Poperinghe	01/07/1917	20/07/1917
War Diary	Winnezeele	21/07/1917	22/07/1917
War Diary	Winnezeele Area	22/07/1917	25/07/1917
War Diary	Watou Area	26/07/1917	30/07/1917
War Diary	Brandhoek.	31/07/1917	31/07/1917
Heading	War Diary. For Month Of August, 1917. Volume 21 Unit 156th Field Company R.E.		
War Diary	Brandhoek	01/08/1917	15/08/1917
War Diary	Vlamertinghe	16/08/1917	19/08/1917

War Diary	Watou	20/08/1917	20/08/1917
War Diary	Eecke	21/08/1917	21/08/1917
War Diary	Bapaume Area	22/08/1917	22/08/1917
War Diary	Gomiecourt	22/08/1917	25/08/1917
War Diary	St. Leger	27/08/1917	31/08/1917
Heading	War Diary. For Month Of September, 1917. Volume 22 Unit- 156th Fd. Co. R.E.		
War Diary	St. Leger	01/09/1917	30/09/1917
Heading	War Diary For Month Of October, 1917. Unit 156th Field Company R.E. Volume Number 23		
War Diary	St Leger	01/10/1917	31/10/1917
Heading	War Diary For Month Of November, 1917. Volume 24 Unit- 156th Field Coy R.E.		
War Diary	St. Leger	01/11/1917	30/11/1917
Heading	War Diary For Month Of December, 1917. Volume 25 Unit 156th Field Coy R.E.		
War Diary	St Leger	01/12/1917	03/12/1917
War Diary	St Leger and Beaulencourt.	04/12/1917	04/12/1917
War Diary	Beaulencourt.	05/12/1917	06/12/1917
War Diary	Tincourt.	06/12/1917	06/12/1917
War Diary	Villers-Faucon	07/12/1917	31/12/1917
Heading	War Diary. For Month Of January, 1918. Volume 26 Unit- 156th Fld. Coy. R.E.		
War Diary	Villers Faucon	01/01/1918	31/01/1918
Heading	War Diary. For Month Of February, 1918. Volume.27 Unit- 156th Field Coy. R.E.		
War Diary	Villers Faucon	01/02/1918	21/02/1918
War Diary	St. Emilie	22/02/1918	28/02/1918
Heading	16th Divisional Engineers 156th Field Company R,E, March 1918		
War Diary	St Emilie	01/03/1918	16/03/1918
War Diary	Villers Faucon	17/03/1918	22/03/1918
War Diary	Villers Faucon and Doigt	22/03/1918	22/03/1918
War Diary	Doigt	23/03/1918	23/03/1918
War Diary	Biaches and Cappy.	23/03/1918	23/03/1918
War Diary	Cappy.	24/03/1918	30/03/1918
War Diary	Hamel.	31/03/1918	31/03/1918
War Diary	Hamel and Aubiany	01/04/1918	01/04/1918
War Diary	Aubigny	02/04/1918	05/04/1918
War Diary	Onicourt (Map:- Abbeville Sheet)	06/04/1918	10/04/1918
War Diary	Woirel (Dieppe Sheet)	11/04/1918	12/04/1918
War Diary	Seux (Amiens Sheet)	13/04/1918	18/04/1918
War Diary	Seux	19/04/1918	30/04/1918
War Diary	Steenbecque	01/05/1918	12/08/1918
War Diary	Clety	12/08/1918	12/08/1918
War Diary	Senelecque	13/08/1918	13/08/1918
War Diary	Lacres.	14/08/1918	21/08/1918
War Diary	Annequin	22/08/1918	31/08/1918
War Diary	Sailly Labourse	01/09/1918	30/09/1918
War Diary	Annequin	01/10/1918	16/10/1918
War Diary	Provin	17/10/1918	18/10/1918
War Diary	Phalempin	19/10/1918	21/10/1918
War Diary	La Posterie	22/10/1918	01/11/1918
War Diary	Taintignies	02/11/1918	08/11/1918
War Diary	Calonne	09/11/1918	12/11/1918
War Diary	ATH	13/11/1918	28/12/1918

War Diary	ATH	15/12/1918	31/12/1918
Heading	War Diary Of The 156th (Field) Coy. R.E. From. 1st. January To 31st January. 1919. Vol 35		
War Diary	A T H	01/01/1919	09/01/1919
War Diary	Barry	10/01/1919	10/01/1919
War Diary	Wez Velvain	11/01/1919	11/01/1919
War Diary	Genech	12/01/1919	12/01/1919
War Diary	Martinsart	13/01/1919	31/01/1919
Heading	War Diary Of The 156th Field Coy R.E From 1st February to 31st February Vol 39		
War Diary	Martinsart	01/02/1919	31/03/1919
Heading	War Diary. 156 Field Coy. R.E. April 1919. Vol 41		
War Diary	Fretin	01/04/1919	22/04/1919
War Diary	X28b 5.9 Factory	23/04/1919	30/04/1919
Heading	War Diary 156 Field Coy. R.E. May. 1919. Vol 42		
War Diary	Fretin X28.b 5.9.	01/05/1919	31/05/1919

(2)

WO 95/1965
16 Division
Headquarters Branches of
Services

Dec 1915 - May 1919

156 Field Company Royal
Engineers.

16TH DIVISION

156TH FIELD COY R.E.
DEC 1915 - MAY 1919

156th R.C.R.E.
Fott: I
Dec.

16th Div.

B.E.F 19.12.15

Dec '15 –
May '19

WAR DIARY or INTELLIGENCE SUMMARY

Army Form C. 2118

156 FIELD COY RE

(Erase heading not required.)

Instructions regarding War Diaries and Intelligence Summaries are contained in F.S. Regs., Part II. and the Staff Manual respectively. Title Pages will be prepared in manuscript.

Place	Date	Hour	Summary of Events and Information	Remarks and references to Appendices
DOVER	29.7.15		W.O. letter O.B/154 (A.G.7) of 27.7.15 directed Captain R.A.W. Marsden R.E. to proceed to CHATHAM with a view to taking command of 156 Field Company R.E. then about to be formed. RM	
CHATHAM	4.8.15 –15.8.15		First draft of Company received from Bulletin Battalion R.E. RM	
"	19.8.15		Three officers, 100 other ranks proceeded to MOORE PARK, KILWORTH. RM	
MOORE PARK	20.8.15 –29.8.15		Further drafts of officers and 105 other ranks, mounted and dismounted received. Carbine musketry instruction and training in pontoon, trestle, and barrel trestle bridging. RM	
"	9.9.15		Company left MOORE PARK. RM	
BLACKDOWN	10.9.15		Company arrived BLACKDOWN hut. RM	
"	10.9.15 –30.10.15		Company being trained under Section Officers, in field work, field defences, saddlery, riding and barrel trestle bridging carried out. Horses and mules received & trained. Equipment being received. Transport (O.R.) horses &c 318. RMS	
"	6.10.15		Lieut W.H. Hunt R.E. arr'd & took over R.E. Stores & Company. W.O. letter O.B/1277 (A.G.7) at 28.9.15. Company now 1 Captain, and 6 Subalterns. RM	
"	30.10.15 31.10.15		Service rifles received. RM	
			6 officers 210 O.R. Marched to HENLEY ON THAMES for pontooning. RM	

O.C. 156th FIELD CO.
CAPT. R.E.

1875 Wt. W593/826 1,000,000 4/15 J.B.C. & A. A.D.S.S./Forms/C. 2118.

WAR DIARY or INTELLIGENCE SUMMARY

Army Form C. 2118

156 FIELD COY RE

Place	Date	Hour	Summary of Events and Information	Remarks and references to Appendices
HENLEY ON THAMES	14.11.15 – 19.11.15		Company in billets. Company being trained in Pontooning. Preliminary musketry training and miniature rifle shooting carried out. RM	
"	16.11.15		On conjunction with 155 Field Coy RE a team pontoon bridge was constructed across the THAMES, about 200 x below HENLEY BRIDGE, on which Q 6.15 motor lorry was passed. G.O.C. 16th Division – Lieut Gen du L. Parriere was present. RM. Company returned to BLACKDOWN. RM	
BLACKDOWN	20.11.15			
"	24.11.15 – 27.11.15		Annual musketry course fired by all ranks & officers at PIRBRIGHT RIFLE RANGE. RM	
"	27–30 "		Organising company into armies and reserve men. RM	

RMW Macnab
CAPT. R.E.
O.C. 156th FIELD CO. R.E.

156 g. eq. Ac.

WAR DIARY or INTELLIGENCE SUMMARY.

156 FIELD COY RE

Army Form C. 2118

(Erase heading not required.)

Place	Date	Hour	Summary of Events and Information	Remarks and references to Appendices
BLACKDOWN	1.12 .15		Senior sections trained by section officers. RVD.	
	—8.12 .15			
	8.12.		Company inspected by Inspector General RE on CHOBHAM RIDGES in review of route. Then was the first parade of the company in uniform, mounted and dismounted. RVD	
	13.12.		Company took part in Divisional Route March. RVD	
	18.12.		Company left BLACKDOWN, marched to FARNBOROUGH (L.S.W.R.), trained to SOUTHAMPTON. Embarked in the afternoon, and crossed over to LE HAVRE at night. RVD	

R W Murcher
Capt.
O.C. 156th FIELD CO. R.E.

WAR DIARY or INTELLIGENCE SUMMARY

Army Form C. 2118

156 FIELD COY RE

(Erase heading not required.)

Place	Date	Hour	Summary of Events and Information	Remarks and references to Appendices
HAVRE	19.12.15	A.M.	Company arrived at HAVRE. Disembarked and proceeded to DOCKS REST CAMP.	
"	20.12.15	A.M.	Left HAVRE by train.	
"	21.12.15	A.M.	Arrived CHOCQUES. Proceeded by road to NOEUX LES MINES, and went into billets in town along the BETHUNE ROAD.	
NOEUX LES MINES	22.12.15		Company employed on stable building for its animals.	
"	23.12.15		Company employed as above. Officers arranged details for further work.	
"	24.12.15		No 4 Section worked at huts for 16th Division Headquarters at BRUVIN. Rem aide on R.E. Scale	
"	25.12.15		As for 24.12.15	
"	26.12.15		1 Section worked with 11th Hampshire Pioneers at FOSSE 6. 2+4 Sections worked at huts at Division Headquarters. 3 Section worked at R.E. Scale.	
"	27.12.15		As for 26.12.15	
"	28.12.15		1 + 3 Sections working at FOSSE 6. 2+4 at Division Headquarters.	
"	29.12.15		As for 28.12.15	
"	30.12.15		As for 29.12.15	
"	31.12.15		As for 30.12.15	

R.M.W. Thunder
Captl
O.C. 156 Field Coy RE

156th F.C. R.E.
vol: 2
Jan '16

16th Div

Army Form C. 2118

WAR DIARY
~~INTELLIGENCE SUMMARY~~
(Erase heading not required.)

156 FIELD COY R.E.

Place	Date	Hour	Summary of Events and Information	Remarks and references to Appendices
NOEUX LES MINES	1.1.16		1 & 3 Sections at work at FOSSE 6. 2 & 4 Sections moved to CHATEAU DROUVIN and hutted there to construct work at hutments. RM	
"	2.1.16		As for 1.1.16 RM	
"	3.1.16		No 2 & 4 Section returned to company headquarters. RM	47th Division S Coll
"	4.1.16		Occupied CHATEAU DROUVIN. RM	
"	5.1.16		As for 4.1.16 RM	
"	6.1.16		As for 5.1.16 RM	
"	7.1.16		As for 6.1.16. O.C. Coy took over hutments at NOEUX LES MINES from 11th Hants RM and carried over work at FOSSE 6 to 138 Army Troop Coy R.E.	
"	8.1.16		Nos 1 & 3 preparing for work at hutments. 2 & 4 completed work at DROUVIN. RM	
"	9.1.16		Whole company commenced work at NOEUX hutments. RM	
"	10.1.16		As for 9.1.16 RM	
"	11.1.16		As for 10.1.16 RM	
"	12.1.16		As for 11.1.16 RM	
"	13.1.16		As for 12.1.16 RM	
"	14.1.16		As for 13.1.16 RM	
"	15.1.16		As for 14.1.16 RM	
"	16.1.16		As for 15.1.16 RM	
"	17.1.16		As for 16.1.16 RM	

RM Rawson
Capt
151 1/16 Fd Coy

Army Form C. 2118

WAR DIARY
or
INTELLIGENCE SUMMARY
(Erase heading not required.)

Instructions regarding War Diaries and Intelligence Summaries are contained in F.S. Regs., Part II. and the Staff Manual respectively. Title Pages will be prepared in manuscript.

Place	Date	Hour	Summary of Events and Information	Remarks and references to Appendices
NOEUX LES MINES	18.1.16		No 1 Section at work at FOSSE 3 de NOEUX, levelling slag heaps. Remainder at work at NOEUX Puitments. R.M.	
"	19.1.16		ditto for 19.1.16 R.M.	
"	20.1.16		Set at work on Puitments M2	
"	21.1.16		ditto for 21.1.16 R.M.	
"	22.1.16		ditto for 22.1.16 R.M.	
"	23.1.16		ditto for 23.1.16 R.M.	
"	24.1.16		ditto for 24.1.16 R.M.	
"	25.1.16		ditto for 25.1.16 R.M.	
"	26.1.16		ditto for 26.1.16 R.M.	
"	27.1.16		ditto for 27.1.16 R.M.	
"	28.1.16		ditto for 28.1.16 R.M.	
"	29.1.16		ditto for 29.1.16 R.M.	
"	30+31.1.16		ditto for 30 + 31.1.16 R.M.	

R.M.W. Marston
Captn
OC 156 Field Coy RE

156 Field / R8

Vol III

16

Army Form C. 2118

WAR DIARY
or
INTELLIGENCE SUMMARY
(Erase heading not required.)

Instructions regarding War Diaries and Intelligence Summaries are contained in F.S. Regs., Part II and the Staff Manual respectively. Title Pages will be prepared in manuscript.

156 FIELD CO/ R E

Place	Date	Hour	Summary of Events and Information	Remarks and references to Appendices
NOEUX LES MINES	1.2.16		Company at work constructing huttments at NOEUX. Rm	
—	2.2.16		do for 1.2.16 Rm	
—	3.2.16		do for 2.2.16 Rm	
—	4.2.16		do for 3.2.16 Rm	
—	5.2.16		do for 4.2.16 Rm	
—	6.2.16		do for 5.2.16 Rm	
—	7.2.16		do for 6.2.16 Rm	
—	8.2.16		do for 7.2.16 Rm	
—	9.2.16		do for 8.2.16 Am	
—	10.2.16		do for 9.2.16 Rm	
—	11.2.16		do for 10.2.16 Rm	
—	12.2.16		do for 11.2.16 Am	
—	13.2.16		Handed over work at NOEUX huttments to 25 A.T.C. R.E. Rm Evacuating and checking stores. Packing regimental kindal. Rm	
—	14.2.16		Transport proceeded by route mar via BETHUNE, CHOCQUES, LILLERS, AUCHY AU BOIS, WESTREHEM, FIEBUIN PALFART, FLECHIN to billets at CUHEM. Dismounted personnel proceeded by train from NOEUX LES MINES to LILLERS, thence by route mar via ECQUEDECQUES, AUCHY AU BOIS, LIGNY-LEZ-AIRE, FEBUIN PALFART, FLECHIN, to billets at CUHEM. Rm	
—	15.2.16		Rm	

1875 Wt. W593/825 1,000,000 4/15 J.B.C. & A. A.D.S.S./Forms/C. 2118.

Army Form C. 2118

WAR DIARY
or
INTELLIGENCE SUMMARY
(Erase heading not required.)

Instructions regarding War Diaries and Intelligence Summaries are contained in F.S. Regs., Part II. and the Staff Manual respectively. Title Pages will be prepared in manuscript.

Place	Date	Hour	Summary of Events and Information	Remarks and references to Appendices
CUHEM	16.2.16		Company employed in cleaning up billeting area, and preparing for inspection by G.O.C. 16th Division Rm.	
"	17.2.16		do for 16.2.16 Rm	
"	18.2.16		Company inspected by Major General W.B. HICKIE. C.B. G.O.C. 16th Division Rm.	
"	19.2.16		Company training under Section Officers. Rm	
"	20.2.16		do for 19.2.16 Rm	
"	21.2.16		Inspection by Lieut. General Sir H. GOUGH, G.O.C. 1st Corps. Rm	
"	22.2.16		Company working at trestle bridging, and laying out hurdles, and demolition Rm	
"	23.2.16		do for 22.2.16. 24 men from 48 INF. BDE. arrived for training as a Brigade Pioneer Platoon. Rm.	
"	24.2.16		Company on scheme with 48 INF. BDE. Combat exercise, night bridging and laying out hurdles practised Rm	
"	25.2.16		Company training Rm.	
"	26.2.16		LIEUT DOYLE and 5 O.R. sent to report K.C.R.E. 33rd DIVN. for finding billets for Company. Rm	
CUHEM	27.2.16		Company proceeded by route march to LA MIQUELLERIE to billets Rm	
LA MIQUELLERIE	28.2.16		Company proceeded by route march to BEUVRY, for attachment to 33rd DIVN.	
BEUVRY	29.2.16		Company employing horse line and billets, arranging and 212 and 222 F.S. COY about other work Rm	

R.M.W. Rawden Cy/126
29.2.16 O.C. 156 F.A. Coy R.E.

Vaal (1)

Passed to you as
these seem to be an
original drawings

W.A. Harrison
Lt Col RE
4/4/16   for RE Rec'd

Vol 4
15 र ह 25।
उर ह रु

Army Form C. 2118

WAR DIARY
or
INTELLIGENCE SUMMARY

(Erase heading not required.)

Instructions regarding War Diaries and Intelligence Summaries are contained in F.S. Regs., Part II. and the Staff Manual respectively. Title Pages will be prepared in manuscript.

156 FIELD COY R.E.

Place	Date	Hour	Summary of Events and Information	Remarks and references to Appendices
BEUVRY	1.3.16	—	Company training for work in Reserve line. O.C. and officer visited hostile wire and other 7 212 Fd Coy R.E. and O.R. over Reserve line.	
"	2.3.16	10 a.m	Wire received from H.Q. 33rd Divn ordering 156 Coy to 1st Divn at BRAQUEMONT on 3.3.16. Arrangements for work made on previous day cancelled. 2/Lieut Cowan proceeded to BRAQUEMONT and arranged billets. Company packing up.	Rm
BRAQUE MONT	3.3.16		Company proceeded to BRAQUEMONT by route march. O.C. reported to 1st Division to arrange for work.	Rm
"	4.3.16		1 officer proceeded with to LES BREBIS to arrange billets for company. O.C. proceeded and O.C. Lowland Fd Coy R.E. at night to inspect DOUBLE CRASSIER.	Rm
LES BREBIS	5.3.16		Company proceeded by route march to LES BREBIS. No1 Section commenced work at night until to trenches held Coy R.E. on Northern arm.) DOUBLE CRASSIER.	Rm
"	6.3.16		No1 Section at night work constructing machine gun emplacement on Northern arm) DOUBLE CRASSIER	Rm
"	7.3.16		No 3 Section constructing light railway LES BREBIS – LOOS. No 2 Section at night work on DOUBLE CRASSIER. No 4 Section constructing M.G. emplacements in front line of 2nd INF. BDE.	Rm
"	8.3.16		As for 7.3.16	Rm

Army Form C. 2118

WAR DIARY
INTELLIGENCE SUMMARY
(Erase heading not required.)

156 FIELD COY R.E.

Instructions regarding War Diaries and Intelligence Summaries are contained in F.S. Regs., Part II. and the Staff Manual respectively. Title Pages will be prepared in manuscript.

Place	Date	Hour	Summary of Events and Information	Remarks and references to Appendices
LES BREBIS	9/3/16		No 1 Section making M.G. emplacements and repairing trench on NORTHERN ARM, DOUBLE CRASSIER. No 3 Section at M.G. emplacements in front line near HARRISON'S CRATER. RM	
	10/3/16		One Section on trench tramway LES BRE B/S - LOOS. One Section making M.G. emplacement and repairing trench on NORTHERN ARM, DOUBLE CRASSIER. One Section making M.G. emplacements in front line near HARRISON'S CRATER. RM	
	11/3/16		As for 10.3.16 RM	
	12/3/16		As for 11.3.16 RM	
	13/3/16		As for 12.3.16. 4 M.G. emplacements in LOOS SECTOR, near indus contained one mile trench railway laid, one M.G. empl. in DOUBLE CRASSIER commenced and carried on when it was practicable to depart. DOUBLE CRASSIER and approach continually being damaged by enemy and repaired by 156 Coy RM	
	14/3/16		Company ordered to rejoin 16th DIVn. at LAPUGNOY. A working party sent off. RM	
LAPUGNOY	15.3.16		Company proceeded to LAPUGNOY, billeted with 48 INF. BDE. RM	
"	16.3.16		Company improving stables and huts. recorded. RM	
"	17.3.16		As for 16.3.16 RM	

Army Form C. 2118

WAR DIARY
or
INTELLIGENCE SUMMARY
(Erase heading not required.)

156 FIELD COY R.E.

Place	Date	Hour	Summary of Events and Information	Remarks and references to Appendices
LAPUGNOY	18.3.16		Company improving platform at No 18 Casualty Clearing Station, carrying out musketry instruction and wire entanglement drill. RM	
"	19.3.16		Rest day. RM	
"	20.3.16		Company training in musketry, wire entanglement, nodding and driving. RM Ditto for 20.3.16. Ditto instruction in bombing. RM	
"	21.3.16		Ditto for 21.3.16. RM	
"	22.3.16		2/Lieut SHELLEY and section proceeded to PHILOSOPHE to take over work on M.G. emplacements in HULLUCH SECTOR from 74th F.D. COY R.E. CAPTAIN HUNT and Stoneman proceeded to PHILOSOPHE to take over Divisional dump at FOSSE 3 from 91st F.D. COY R.E. RM	
"	23.3.16		O.C. Company proceeded to PHILOSOPHE to take over HULLUCH SECTOR from O.C. 74 F.D COY R.E. 2/Lieut SHELLEY erected tracks and NCO's of section attached to 74 F.D COY for work. Remainder of Company training at LAPUGNOY. RM	
PHILOSOPHE	24.3.16			
LAPUGNOY	"		Company preparing to move. RM	
"	25.3.16		O.C Company visited handed over to 74 F.D COY R.E.	
PHILOSOPHE	"	5 p.m.	FOSSE 3 Store taken over from 91st FD COY R.E. RM	
"	25/26 m.n.		Commenced work at 2 Artillery exchange dugouts. Took over work from 74 FD COY R.E	
PHILOSOPHE	26/3/16		Remainder of company arrived. The section working in shifts at artillery exchange dug outs.	

Army Form C. 2118

WAR DIARY
~~INTELLIGENCE SUMMARY~~
(Erase heading not required.)

156 FD COY RE

Place	Date	Hour	Summary of Events and Information	Remarks and references to Appendices
PHILOSOPHE	26/3/16	9 p.m.	Two sections sent to kop 9" R.M.F. to repair handles and consolidate crater formed by German mine.	
"	27/3/16		OC visited craters and arranged with OC 9 RMF and GOC 48 INF BDE for work in craters. 1 Section working with 253 Tunnelling Coy on listening gallery. 2 sections employed on repairing parados and consolidating craters. RM	
"	28/3/16		1 Section employed on R.A. exchange dug outs. Sapping up to crater continued. Work on R.A. dugouts and on listening gallery continued. RM.	
"	29/3/16		Sapping to NORTHERN CRATER and lining sapheads completed. Sapping to SOUTHERN CRATER owing to enfiled enemy mining operation. No work possible. Work on R.A. dugout and on listening gallery continued. RM.	
"	30/3/16		Further work on consolidation of craters carried out.	
"	31/3/16		Work on machine gun dugouts and new dug outs commenced. As for 30.3.16.	

R. M. W. Marsden
CAPT. R.E.
O.C. 156th FIELD CO

Daaly (1)

Forwarded as two
War Diaries shown to
be original copies not
Duplicates

W.H. Saum[?]
Lieut [?]
5/5/16   4/Alb[?]

WAR DIARY / INTELLIGENCE SUMMARY

Army Form C. 2118

156 FIELD COY R.E.

Place	Date	Hour	Summary of Events and Information	Remarks and references to Appendices
PHILOSOPHE	1.4.16		Consolidating MUNSTER and TRALEE craters and faults of 7 R.I. Rifles. Making machine gun dug out, bomb store and dug out in SUPPORT TRENCH. Repairing subway/trench. R.M.	
"	2.4.16		Consolidation & craters etc as above. R.M.	
"	3.4.16		As above. R.E. also about and superintendent digging 70 hand bay 8" and 9" R.D.F. across southern front in HULLUCH SECTOR R.M.	
"	4.4.16		Work as for 2.4.16 R.M.	
"	5.4.16		As for 4.4.16 R.D.F. Bomb store completed. Two new M.G. dugouts in reserve line started R.M.	
"	6.4.16		As for 5.4.16. 48 INF.BDE relieved by 47 INF.BDE R.M.	
"	7.4.16		As for 6.4.16. W.H.H.	
"	8.4.16		Changing over took night 157 field Coy. night.	
"	9.4.16		Widening & deepening of communication Trench (French alley). Concreting M.G. emplacement & collecting Tramway. Scrap.	W.H.H.
"	10.4.16		" " " " " " "	W.H.H.
"	11.4.16		" " " " " " repairing bridge "	W.H.H.
"	12.4.16		Construction bridge over communication Trench (French alley). M.G. emplacements. Clearing billets. Collecting Tramway scrap.	W.H.H.
"	13.4.16		Clearing debris, repairing road after shell fire. Construction of bridge over communication trench (French alley). M.G. emplacement. Providing Hurks, hand torches, T.M. Butts & repairing billets.	W.H.H.

WAR DIARY or INTELLIGENCE SUMMARY

Army Form C. 2118

(Erase heading not required.)

Instructions regarding War Diaries and Intelligence Summaries are contained in F.S. Regs., Part II. and the Staff Manual respectively. Title Pages will be prepared in manuscript.

Place	Date	Hour	Summary of Events and Information	Remarks and references to Appendices
Philosophe	14/4/16		Erecting & purchasing platt shelters in billets. Completing Bath house, ketchen and deepening communication from pumping Pit Cln. to los form in an enemy direction. Pallisade wooden paving. Cable laid to M.G. emplacement finished, & mine ball continued. Construction continued in M.G. V.S. & O.P. on top Fose 3	WD/H
Philosophe	15/4/16		Construction O.P. Fose 3. Construction of dugout & re-construction of pump horse Fose 3 work commenced. Ballast loader tramway. Construction M.G. emplacement.	WD/H
"	16/4/16		as for 15/4/16	WD/H
"	17/4/16		as for 16/4/16.	WD/H
"	18/4/16		as for 17/4/16 and construction M.G. emplacement, erecting battomet hut completed	WD/H
"	19/4/16		O.P. Fose 3. 95% completed. M.G. emplacement erecting 80% completed, no work done on account of no fatigue party. Dug out Fose 3. 85% completed, & Pump house 65% completed. No work done on T.M. emplacement & shelters, account no fatigue party.	WD/H
"	20.4.16		O.P. FOSSE 3 completed. Work as for 19.4.16 carried on. Stone for T.M. emplacements conveyed to LOOS, but no work done, owing to hostile shelling of transport. 2/Lieut T.C. Roberts and 2 Sappers wounded.	RM
"	21.4.16		Work as for 20.4.16	RM
"	22.4.16		Work as for 21.4.16. Officers taking over front line system from 155 FD COY RE	RM

Army Form C. 2118
XVI
Vol 5

WAR DIARY
or
INTELLIGENCE SUMMARY
(Erase heading not required.)

156 F.D. COY. R.E.

Place	Date	Hour	Summary of Events and Information	Remarks and references to Appendices
PHILOSOPHE	23/4/16		Work on 14 BIS SECTOR. Relief by 48 INF. BDE. Taken over. RM	
"	24/4/16		Company at work on front line system 14 BIS SECTOR. Work on Rear - construction of dugouts in trench, construction of listening galleries 2 + 3, construction of splinter proof shelters in fire trench and entanglement, construction of small m.g. emplacement in Reserve line. Cleaning fire system and revetting CORK TRENCH, HOHENZ TRENCH, GALWAY TRENCH. RM	
"	25/4/16		As for 24.4.16 RM	
"	26/4/16		As for 25.4.16 RM	
"	27/4/16	5:10 a.m	Enemy made gas attack on 14 BIS SECTOR. Also bombarded PHILOSOPHE with H.E. shrapnel, and tear shell. Effect of this gas felt at PHILOSOPHE. Company working at night clearing front and support lines. RM	
"	28.4.16		Company at work repairing damage done on 27.4.16 RM	
"	29.4.16		Enemy made further gas attack, and bombarded PHILOSOPHE on 27.4.16. Effect of gas not felt at PHILOSOPHE. Direct hit by 8" shell on [illeg] billet. 1 M.G., 2 O.R. severely wounded 1 N.C.O. 3 O.R. Company slightly by and using RM	
"	30.4.16		½ Company employed in further strengthening of billets. ½ Company resumed normal work with trench RM	

R.M.W. Marsden
Capt.
OC 156 Field Coy RE

Army Form C. 2118.

WAR DIARY
or
INTELLIGENCE SUMMARY
(Erase heading not required.)

156 FD COY. R.E. Vol 6

XVI

Place	Date	Hour	Summary of Events and Information	Remarks and references to Appendices
PHILOSOPHE	1.5.16.		Company at work in Trenches. Carrying on with latrine gallerys No 2 & 3 in front line. Making front slope dug out in Support line. Retaining and reconstruction work in CHALK PIT SALIENT. Construction 7 crewed M.G. emplacement and dek dug out in Reserve line. Construction 7 deep dug out in support line. Clearing and widening main alleys from front line to K Village line. RM	
	2.5.16		do for 1.5.16 RM. Also constructing deep dug out for wireless operator in Reserve line RM.	
	3.5.16		do for 2.5.16 RM	
	4.5.16		do for 3.5.16 RM	
	5.5.16		do for 4.5.16 RM	
	6.5.16		do for 5.5.16 RM	
	7.5.16		do for 6.5.16 RM	
	8.5.16		do for 7.5.16 RM	
	9.5.16		OC handed work on dug out in Reserve line to 5" Lates NORTHANTS PIONEERS. Also took party 75 NORTHANTS (P) round works taken on work on communication trenches. RM	
	10.5.16		OC visited HARTS and HARRISON'S CRATERS and CRE 12 DIVN. and OC 26 FD COY RE with Q near LE Lubin our LOOS SECTOR. RM.	

Army Form C. 2118

WAR DIARY
INTELLIGENCE SUMMARY

(Erase heading not required.)   156 FD COY RE

Place	Date	Hour	Summary of Events and Information	Remarks and references to Appendices
PHILOSOPHE	11.5.16		Shelling PHILOSOPHE all day; intense bombardment with 8" howitzer fire and other shells from 3.30 to 6.30 p.m. Much damage done to Kiosk; one man slightly wounded.	RM
	12.5.16		Work as for 1.5.16. Reinforcement with the exception of work parties went to NORTH ANTS (P).	RM
	13.5.16		As for 12.5.16.	RM
	14.5.16		Work as for 13.5.16. Artillery of the other bombarded enemy trenches from 12.30 to 1 p.m. 6.49 p.m. enemy's artillery commenced retaliation.	RM
	15.5.16		Work as for 14.5.16.	RM
	16.5.16		Company handed over work from ENGLISH ALLEY — POSEN ALLEY to 155 FD COY RE and took over from GORDON ALLEY — HAYMARKET from 267 FD COY RE (1st Division) consequent on alteration of Divisional frontiers. 49 INF BDE came up, relieving 47" + 2" INF BDES. Company employed on HARTS and HARRISON'S CRATERS, construction of new traverses in front line near LENS ROAD, deepening infantry trenches, and construction of dug outs.	RM
	17.5.16		Work as for 16.5.16.	RM
	18.5.16		As for 17.5.16.	RM
	19.5.16		As for 18.5.16.	RM

Army Form C. 2118

WAR DIARY
INTELLIGENCE SUMMARY
(Erase heading not required.)

156 FD COY RE

Instructions regarding War Diaries and Intelligence Summaries are contained in F. S. Regs., Part II. and the Staff Manual respectively. Title Pages will be prepared in manuscript.

Place	Date	Hour	Summary of Events and Information	Remarks and references to Appendices
PHILOSOPHE	20.5.16		As for 19.5.16 RM.	
"	21.5.16		Handed over work on front line again to 157 FD Coy, and took over Reserve Coy work from same. RM.	
"	22.5.16		Work on tunnelled M.G. empts in CHALK PIT and RAILWAY ALLEYS; Survey O.P. and R.A. O.P. in CHALK PIT ALLEY; tunnelled tramway V china - Posen: maintenance of trench mortar emplts; protection for Dressing station at PHILOSOPHE; improvement of Rifle Pits. RM.	
	23.5.16		do for 22.5.16 RM.	
	24.5.16		do for 23.5.16 RM.	
	25.5.16		do for 24.5.16 RM.	
	26.5.16		do for 25.5.16 RM.	
	27.5.16		do for 26.5.16. Dressing station completed RM.	
	28.5.16		do for 27.5.16 RM.	
	29 - 31.5.16		do for 28.5.16. RM.	

R.M.W. Marsden
Capt R.E.
O.C. 156 Fd Coy R.E.

DAG 3rd Echelon
GHQ

Herewith War Diary
for June 1916.

R.M.W. Macuen

1 JUL
1 JUL 1916

Army Form C. 2118

Vol 7 June

15t Field Coy R.E.

WAR DIARY
or
INTELLIGENCE SUMMARY
(Erase heading not required.)

Place	Date	Hour	Summary of Events and Information	Remarks and references to Appendices
PHILOSOPHE	1.6.16		Work on water supply (laying pipe line FOSSE 7 & FOSSE 3), making dug out for Survey O.P., ballasting wooden railway VICTORIA STN - POSEN STN, and building M.G. emp[lacemen]ts in CHALKPIT and RAILWAY ALLEYS. Pm.	
	2.6.16		As for 1.6.16. Pm.	
	3.6.16.		Half Company 7/SUFFOLKS (12 DIV) attached for work on dug outs in 65 metre and LENS ROAD REDOUBTS, and A.D.S. in CHALKPIT ALLEY. Handing over Reserve Coy work to 155 Fd Coy. Pm.	
	4.6.16		Took over work on front line system 14 Bis SECTOR, occupied by 47/I.B. Work carried on L.G. 16 + 19, and dug outs in front line system. Pm.	
	5.6.16		As for 4.6.16. Pm.	
	6.6.16		As for 5.6.16. Pm.	
	7.6.16		As for 6.6.16. Also work on opening up BROADWAY and trench from H.Q. c.3.9.b.5 H.2.5 a 3.9. Pm.	
	8.6.16		As for 7.6.16. Pm.	
	9.6.16		As for 8.6.16. Listening galleries 16 + 17 completed. Pm.	
	10.6.16		As for 9.6.16. 49 INF. BDE. relieved 47th in 14 Bis SECTOR. Pm	
	11.6.16		Work as for 10.6.16. T.C. 27 + 28 started. Pm.	
	12.6.16		As for 11.6.16. Pm.	

Army Form C. 2118

WAR DIARY
or
INTELLIGENCE SUMMARY
(Erase heading not required.)

156 Fd Coy R.E.

Instructions regarding War Diaries and Intelligence Summaries are contained in F. S. Regs., Part II. and the Staff Manual respectively. Title Pages will be prepared in manuscript.

Place	Date	Hour	Summary of Events and Information	Remarks and references to Appendices
PHILOSOPHE	13.6		At fr 12.6.16 PM	
	14.6		At fr 13.6.16 PM	
	15-6 / 16 / 17 / 18.6		} Company employed on special work in Fire trench PM	
	19.6		Normal work resumed PM	
	20.6		At fr 19.6 PM	
	21.6		At fr 20.6 PM	
	22.6		At fr 21.6 PM	
	23.6		At fr 22.6 PM } 229 Fd Coy R.E. (40 OR) attached for instruction, and put on deep dug out and finishing PM	
	24.6		At fr 23.6 PM }	
	25.6		No work attached E ¬ VILLAGE LINE. Coy at work finishing NORTHERN SAP REDOUBT. 229 Coy dugout in NORTHERN SAP REDOUBT. 24 OR 156 Fd Coy lent to C Coy 4/8" Staffs Bde R.E. PM.	
	26.6		At fr 25.6. 48 INF BDE relieved 49 INF BDE in 14 BIS. SECTOR PM	
	27.6		Work on dug out in RESERVE, MEATH, SUPPORT & FIRE TRENCHES carried out by 156 Coy. Also L.G. 37 & 38. 229 Coy left of NORTHERN SAP REDOUBT PM	
	28.6		At fr 27.6. PM.	
	29.6		At fr 28.6. PM	
	30.6		At fr 29.6. PM	

R.M.W. Murdoch
CAPT RE
OC 156 Fd Coy RE

WAR DIARY

156th Field Coy
Royal Engineers

1st. July to 31st. July 1916.

VOLUME NO. 8

Army Form C. 2118

WAR DIARY
or
~~INTELLIGENCE SUMMARY~~

156 Field Coy R.E.

(Erase heading not required.)

Instructions regarding War Diaries and Intelligence Summaries are contained in F.S. Regs, Part II. and the Staff Manual respectively. Title Pages will be prepared in manuscript.

Place	Date	Hour	Summary of Events and Information	Remarks and references to Appendices
PHILOSOPHE	1.7.16		Company making dug outs in front line system 14 BIS SECTOR and water supply system from FOSSE 3. FOSSE 7 to 10" Avenue. R.m.	
	2.7.16		Jb for 1.7.16. R.m.	
	3.7.16		Jb for 2.7.16. R.m.	
	4.7.16		Started own work on front line system of 157 Fd C.R.E. VE and V6. Took over work on M.G. emplt in VILLAGE LINE (14 BIS SECTOR); built O.P. (GAIETY) at MAROC for R.A.; dugout in 65 METRE POINT REDOUBT and sunray dug out; laid out new dugout in NORTHERN SAP REDOUBT. R.m. Work on provision store LEN'S ROAD REDOUBT. R.m.	
	5.7.16		Work as for 4.7.16. R.m.	
	6.7.16		Work as for 5.7.16. R.m. Sunray still in NOEUX LES MINES and conducting newcastle. R.m.	
	7.7.16		Provision store LENS ROAD REDOUBT completed. Roof of M.G. V5 completed. Work as for 6.7.16 R.m.	
	8.7.16		Work as for 7.7.16. R.m.	
	9.7.16		Jb for 8.7.16. R.m.	
	10.7.16		One dug out in NORTHERN SAP REDOUBT completed. Trench for water supply to NORTHERN SAP REDOUBT dug. Other work as for 9.7.16. R.m.	
	11.7.16		Work as for 10.7.16. R.m.	
	12.7.16		Jb for 11.7.16. R.m.	

Army Form C. 2118

Instructions regarding War Diaries and Intelligence Summaries are contained in F. S. Regs., Part II. and the Staff Manual respectively. Title Pages will be prepared in manuscript.

WAR DIARY
or
INTELLIGENCE SUMMARY
(Erase heading not required.)

156 FIELD COY. R.E.

Place	Date	Hour	Summary of Events and Information	Remarks and references to Appendices
PHILOSOPHE	13.7.16		Handed over 2 dug outs in NORTHERN JAP REDOUBT & WHTOME COUNTIES F.D. COY. R.E. Commenced work on front close under FOSSE 3. RM	
"	14.7.16		As for 13.7.16. A.M. completed new alibi at NOEUX LES MINES. RM	
"	15.7.16		Completed GAIETY O.P. MAROC. Completed Raying on wall to NORTHERN JAP REDOUBT. Completed MC V5 and V6 ready for table. Completed survey of dug out near G5 mine front whart RM	
"	16.7.16		Handed over Reserve Coy work to 155 Fd Coy R.E. Took over front line system, LOOS SECTOR from 155 Fd Coy R.E. 49 INF BDE in the line. 2 Sections billeted in HIGH ST. LOOS. 1 Section working on HART'S CRATER 1 on HARRISON'S CRATER, 1 on SEAFORTH CRATERS. 1 on dug out construction. RM	
"	17.7.16		As for 16.7.16 RM	
"	18.7.16		As for 17.7.16 RM	
"	19.7.16		As for 18.7.16. 48 INF. BDE. relieved 49 INF. BDE. RM	
"	20.7.16		As for 19.7.16. RM	
"	21.7.16		O.C. Company took on R.E. work on HULLUCH SECTOR from 73RD FD COY R.E. RM	
"	22.7.16		Handed over LOOS SECTOR to 224 F.D.COY. R.E. for (40 DIVN) 2 Sections moved from tools to THIBAULT THE ASYLUM & THIBAULT (15 DIVN) 2 Section started work on HULLUCH CRATERS and GREEN QUAVE. 49 INF BDE in line. RM	

Army Form C. 2118

WAR DIARY or INTELLIGENCE SUMMARY

(Erase heading not required.)

156 FD COY RE

Instructions regarding War Diaries and Intelligence Summaries are contained in F.S. Regs., Part II. and the Staff Manual respectively. Title Pages will be prepared in manuscript.

Place	Date	Hour	Summary of Events and Information	Remarks and references to Appendices
PHILOSOPHE	23.7.16		2 Sections at work on HULLUCH CRATER defences, GREEN CURVE and front and support line in neighbourhood. 1 Section futurity R.E. accommodation near "I" [Spinney?]. 1 in Reserve. RM	
	24.7.16		As for 23.7.16 RM. 48 INF BDE relieved 49 INF BDE. RM	
	25.7.16		2 Sections working on HULLUCH CRATER defences, GREEN CURVE and front line in neighbourhood. Remainder preparing R.E. accommodation in LONE TRENCH and constructing bridges over trenches for wheeled transport. RM	
	26.7.16		As for 25.7.16 RM	
	27.7.16		As for 26.7.16 RM	
	28.7.16		As for 27.7.16 RM	
	29.7.16		As for 28.7.16 Bridges completed. RM	
	30.7.16		Night work on craters prevented by trench being reserved for carrying parties. Section employed on normal work, also on cleaning and fitting equipment ready for use. RM	
	31.7.16		Normal work.	

R.M.W. Marden
CAPT
OC 156 Fd Coy RE

1/8/16

Vol 9

WAR DIARY.

156th Field Coy R.E.

MONTH OF AUGUST, 1916.

VOLUME:- 9.

Army Form C. 2118

WAR DIARY
INTELLIGENCE SUMMARY
(Erase heading not required.)

156 FIELD Coy R.E.

Instructions regarding War Diaries and Intelligence Summaries are contained in F. S. Regs., Part II. and the Staff Manual respectively. Title Pages will be prepared in manuscript.

Place	Date	Hour	Summary of Events and Information	Remarks and references to Appendices
PHILOSOPHE	1.8.16		Work north 48 INF BDE in line in HULLUCH SECTOR, VENDIN ALLEY to HULLUCH ROAD. Company employed in consolidating HULLUCH CRATERS, finishing and improving GREEN CURVE, constructing dugout for R.E. in LOVE TRENCH. R.m.	
	2.8.16		As for 1.8.16 R.m.	
	3.8.16		Also construction of M.G. dugouts R₂ + R₃ and laying on water & road opposite FOSSE 3 R.m	
	4.8.16		As for 3.8.16 R.m	
	5.8.16		As for 4.8.16 R.m	
	6.8.16		Water laid on. Other work as for 5.8.16 R.m.	
	7.8.16		Work on R.E. dugouts handed over to 155 Fd Coy R.E. Coy officers taking over work in LOOS SECTOR from 224 Fd Coy R.E. (40" Divn). Other work as on 6.8.16 R.m	
	8.8.16		Work on GREEN CURVE and HULLUCH CRATERS handed over to 155 Fd Co R.E. 2 Section sent to Billet in LOOS. R.m	
	9.8.16		47 INF. BDE. took over LOOS SECTOR from 120 INF. BDE. R.m	
	10.8.16		Work on dugout in billet and Repair lines, work on HARRISON'S, HART'S and SEAFORTH CRATERS, work on shelter in front line right subsection. Work on FOSSE 7 pumping station. R.m	

Army Form C. 2118

WAR DIARY
or
INTELLIGENCE SUMMARY
(Erase heading not required.)

1st FC 37 RE

Instructions regarding War Diaries and Intelligence Summaries are contained in F. S. Regs., Part II. and the Staff Manual respectively. Title Pages will be prepared in manuscript.

Place	Date	Hour	Summary of Events and Information	Remarks and references to Appendices
PHILOSOPHE	11.8.16		As on 10.8.16. RM. Also work on M.G. R 6 A cmplt. RM	
	12.8.16		As on 11.8.16. Also work on medium T.M. emplacement supporting new GORDON and SEAFORTH ALLEYS and work on improvement of infantry trench in PHILOSOPHE WEST. RM.	
	13.8.16		As for 12.9.16 RM	
	14.8.16		As for 13.8.16. Work on M.G. R 6 A completed RM.	
	15.8.16		As for 14.8.16. RM.	
	16.8.16		As for 15.8.16 RM.	
	17.8.16		As for 16.8.16. Also work on new emplacement for heavy T.M. near HAY HILL commenced. RM	
	18.8.16		As for 17.8.16. RM.	
	19.8.16		As for 18.8.16 RM.	
	20.8.16		As for 19.8.16. RM.	
	21.8.16 2.a.m		Mine exploded by us then enemy's consolidation on HARRISON'S CRATER. Party under 2/Lt HICKSON R.E. consisted of 1 other rank and 1 off. 25 O.R. 6 R.I. Regt, for consolidating and wiring. Very little damage done to our consolidation, which was put into soon. No mining done. Other work as usual on 21.8.16 RM.	
	22.8.16		Usual work in land. RM. Secret orders received to be prepared to move on 24". RM	
	23.8.16		Usual work in hand, secret orders received to prepared to move on 24th RM. Work on dug out and PHILOSOPHE W. 2 forward section withdrawn from LOOS RM	

1875 Wt. W593/826 1,000,000 4/15 J.B.C. & A. A.D.S.S./Forms/C. 2118.

Army Form C. 2118.

152 FD. COY. R.E.

WAR DIARY
INTELLIGENCE SUMMARY.
(Erase heading not required.)

Place	Date	Hour	Summary of Events and Information	Remarks and references to Appendices
RUITZ	24.8.16		Company proceeded by march to RUITZ. P.m.	
	25.8.16		Company proceeded by march route from RUITZ to HURIONVILLE, billeted with 47 INF. BDE. P.m.	
HURIONVILLE	26.8.16		Company resting, cleaning horses, etc. A.m.	
	27.8.16		A/m 26.8.16 absent P.m.	
	28.8.16		A/m 27.8.16 after rifle & revolver drill contacting. P.m.	
	29.8.16		Proceeded by march route to FOUQUEREIL. P.m.	
	30.8.16		Entrained FOUQUEREIL. Proceeded to LONGUEAU by train. Marched from LONGUEAU to DAOURS. Billetted DAOURS. P.m. 823 N.E. F15 C. R.m.	
	31.8.16		Proceeded by march route to CITADEL camping area. 823 N.E. F15 C. R.m.	

R.M.W. Rowles
C.M.P.R.
OC 152 Fd Coy RE

WAR DIARY

156th Field Company R.E.

FOR MONTH OF SEPTEMBER, 1916.

VOLUME 10

Army Form C. 2118.

WAR DIARY or INTELLIGENCE SUMMARY.

156 F.S. Coy R.E.

(Erase heading not required.)

Instructions regarding War Diaries and Intelligence Summaries are contained in F.S. Regs., Part II. and Staff Manual respectively. Title pages will be prepared in manuscript.

Place	Date	Hour	Summary of Events and Information	Remarks and references to Appendices
CITADEL	1.9.16		Company in bivouacs resting. R.A.	
"	2.9.16		Engaged on improvement to Company grounds. R.M.	
"	3.9.16		1 Sect. Company ordered to be ready to move at 3 hours notice. R.M.	
"	4.9.16		do to 3.9.16. Moved to BILLON FARM. R.M.	
BILLON FARM	5.9.16		Coys. Reserve. O.C. & Officers visited line. R.M.	
"	6.9.16		Moved to MINDEN PIT. Moved on to CRATERS & bivouac. Relieved 155 Fd. Coy in the line. Two sections sent to GUILLEMONT to assist 48 INF BDE in consolidating position on left flank of GUILLEMONT which was on ground by enemy during 20" DIV'S push. GINCHY. R.M.	
CARNOY	7.9.16	4.30 a.m.	Two sections sent up to relieve sections at GUILLEMONT. Coy H.Q. moved to CARNOY.	
GUILLEMONT		5.30 p.m.	Transport and half Coy. to MINDEN POINT. Remainder of Company proceeded to GUILLEMONT to garrison GUILLEMONT and to carry on constn. of new O.P. & 11" Hand. Grenades. R.M.	
GUILLEMONT	8.9.16		Carried on work of consolidating GUILLEMONT & arrangements made for attack on GINCHY. Coy placed at disposal of 48 INF BDE for attack on GINCHY on 9.9.16. R.M.	

Army Form C. 2118.

WAR DIARY
INTELLIGENCE SUMMARY
(Erase heading not required.)

156 FIELD Co RE

Instructions regarding War Diaries and Intelligence Summaries are contained in F.S. Regs., Part II. and Staff Manual respectively. Title pages will be prepared in manuscript.

Place	Date	Hour	Summary of Events and Information	Remarks and references to Appendices
GUILLEMONT	9.9.16	7 a.m.	Intense heavy bombardment by British on enemy front.	
		10.15 a.	2 sections sent forward to join 8" & 9" R.D.F. in forward trench.	
			2 sections held in reserve at GUILLEMONT QUARRY.	
		4.45 p.m.	Infantry advanced to attack GINCHY. 2 sections advanced behind infantry to consolidate captured positions. Attack successful but left flank refused. Kept WEDGE 156c.	
			held clear and reorganised defences on left.	
		6.30 p.m.	1 drum section sent up to left flank.	
		7.30 p.m.	Last ration also sent up.	
	10.9.16	3.30 a.m.	Consolidation of left and right flanks carried out till relieved by 1st Welsh Guards Nov. R.E. northwards to GUILLEMONT.	
			Coy marched to MINDEN POINT. Thence to billets at MORLANCOURT on	
VAUX	11.9.16		Coy marched to bivouac at VAUX from SOMME Rn.	
	12.9.16		Coy from bivouacked at VAUX Rn.	
	13.9.16		Company at VAUX training and outfitting Rn.	
	14.9.16		Ditto Rn.	
	15.9.16		Ditto Rn.	

Army Form C. 2118.

WAR DIARY
INTELLIGENCE SUMMARY.
(Erase heading not required.)

Instructions regarding War Diaries and Intelligence Summaries are contained in F. S. Regs., Part II. and the Staff Manual respectively. Title pages will be prepared in manuscript.

15ᵗ FIELD CO RE

Place	Date	Hour	Summary of Events and Information	Remarks and references to Appendices
VAUX	16.9.16		As for 15.9.16 Rm	
"	17.9.16		Mounted personnel and transport proceeded to PICQUIGNY: dismounted remained at VAUX in bivouac Rm	
HUPPY	18.9.16		Mounted personnel and transport proceeded to HUPPY: dismounted personnel by bus to HUPPY Rm	
"	19.9.16		Billeted at HUPPY. Company training and cleaning up Rm kits Rm	
"	20.9.16			
"	21.9.16		Proceeded by road route to ABBEVILLE, and entrained at ABBEVILLE Rm	
METEREN	22.9.16		Detrained BAILLEUL. Marched to METEREN to billet. Rm Joined IX Corps personal Army Rm	
"	23.9.16		Company at METEREN Rm	
"	24.9.16		Company marched to camp at road SCHERPENBERG- LA CLYTTE Rm	
SCHERPENBERG	25.9.16		Company improvements to camp and stable, and working at 47 INF BDE Hd.qr Rm	
"	26.9.16		Company building stable for 2 Camps and improving 47 INF BDE HQr Rm	
"	27.9.16		As for 26.9.16 Rm	
"	28.9.16		As for 27.9.16 Rm	
"	29.9.16		As for 28.9.16. Also commenced bomb store at SCHERPENBERG. Rm	
"	30.9.16		As for 29.9.16 Rm	

W A R   D I A R Y

MONTH   OF   OCTOBER,   1916.

VOLUME No. 11

156th Field Co. R.E.

Army Form C. 2118.

WAR DIARY
or
INTELLIGENCE SUMMARY
(Erase heading not required.)

156 FIELD CO R E

October 1916

Place	Date	Hour	Summary of Events and Information	Remarks and references to Appendices
SCHERPENBERG	1.10.16		Work on horse lines for 156 and 157 Coys. Existing Divisional Bomb store at SCHERPENBERG. RM. Also improvements to 47 INF BDE Hdqrs. RM.	
"	2.10.16		As for 1.10.16 RM	
"	3.10.16		Coy relieved 3 Coy 11" HANTS (T) in the line, and attached to 47 INF BDE for work. Moved to R.C. FARM, leaving transport at SCHERPENBERG. Handed over work to D Coy 11" HANTS (T). Commenced taking instruction in wiring for 47 INF BDE pm.	
R.C. FARM	4.10.16		Coy at work on new support line W. of VANDENBERGE FM, new communication trench N18 C4.3 to N18 C1.4, and minor drainage repairs RM.	
"	5.10.16		As for 4.10.16. Also work on wiring further of front line RM.	
"	6.10.16		As for 5.10.16. Also work at Bde Hqr, ICHERTENBERG, improvements to infantry billets at SIEGE FM and SANDBAG VILLA RM.	
"	7.10.16		As for 6.10.16. Also work on improving company billet R.C. FARM. RM	
"	8.10.16		As for 7.10.16 RM	
"	9.10.16		As for 8.10.16 RM	
"	10.10.16		As for 9.10.16 RM	
"	11.10.16		One section sent back to SCHERPENBERG for work on hutting under C.R.E. RM	

Army Form C. 2118.

WAR DIARY
INTELLIGENCE SUMMARY.
(Erase heading not required.)

156 FIELD COY R.E.

Instructions regarding War Diaries and Intelligence Summaries are contained in F. S. Regs., Part II. and the Staff Manual respectively. Title pages will be prepared in manuscript.

Place	Date	Hour	Summary of Events and Information	Remarks and references to Appendices
R.C. FARM	12.10.16		Coy Company 11th HANTS (D) found under 156 Coy R.E. for work. R.E. work as before. HANTS at work on sunning up K13 front line and K 13 A. Rm.	
"	13.10.16		As for 12.10.16 Rm	
"	14.10.16		Do for 13.10.16 Rm	
"	15.10.16		Do for 14.10.16. Rm	
"	16.10.16		Do for 15.10.16 Rm	
"	17.10.16		Do for 16.10.16 Rm	
"	18.10.16		Do for 17.10.16 Rm	
"	19.10.16		Do for 18.10.16 Rm	
"	20.10.16		Do for 19.10.16. Also started drying room at YORK HOUSE Rd	
"	21.10.16		Do for 20.10.16 Rm	
"	22.10.16		Do for 21.10.16. Rm.	
"	23.10.16		Section of the LON CAMP brought up, and author sent back to whence from C.S.O. I visited Kinda and asked 215th Heavy T.M. Emplacement. Rm went to a 23A. Heavy T.M. Empt. not out Rm	
"	24.10.16			
"	25.10.16		Work on Heavy T.M. Emplt. started Rm	

Army Form C. 2118.

WAR DIARY

~~INTELLIGENCE~~ SUMMARY. 156 FIELD COY. R.E

(Erase heading not required.)

Instructions regarding War Diaries and Intelligence Summaries are contained in F. S. Regs., Part II. and the Staff Manual respectively. Title pages will be prepared in manuscript.

Place	Date	Hour	Summary of Events and Information	Remarks and references to Appendices
PIOEGE @ PM	26/10		do for 25.10 PM	
	27/10		do for 26.10 PM	
	28/10		do for 27.10 PM	
	29/10		No night work owing to road made by 49 INF BDE PM	
	30.10		Work on 28.10 Trench undermined by hostile artillery restarted on 29.10 PM	
	31.10		do for 30.10 PM	

R.M.W Moore

WAR DIARY.

FOR

MONTH OF NOVEMBER, 1916.

VOLUME 12.

156th Field Coy. R.E.

Vol 12

WAR DIARY

INTELLIGENCE SUMMARY

(Erase heading not required.)

Army Form C. 2118.

156 FQ GR

Place	Date 1916	Hour	Summary of Events and Information	Remarks and references to Appendices
Ploeg Fm.	1/11		1 Section at DE ZON Camp for bathing etc. 3 Section working in FRONT LINE. NEW SUPPORT LINE. CORK TRENCH. D Coy 11 North Pioneers working on BIRR TRENCH. A.C.	
	2/11		As for 1/11/16 Conferred with Lt. Col. MONTEAGLE BROWN respecting patrol on PETIT BOIS A.C.	
	3/11		As for 2/11/16 A.C.	
	4/11		As for 3/11/16 A.C. Prepared BANGALORE TORPEDOES for raid. C.S.M. sent to hospital A.C.	
	5/11		As for 4/11/16 Two emplacements built for STOKES GUN A.C.	
	6/11		As for 5/11/16 Two emplacements built by 47 Bde. Demonstrates use of BANGALORE TORPEDO to infantry. 2 NCO's and 10 Sappers accompany infantry on raid as Demolition party A.C. Lt SKIPPER sent to hospital with jaundice A.C.	
	7/11		As for 5/11/16 A.C.	
	8/11		As for 7/11/16 Section at DE ZON Camp relieved A.C.	
	9/11		As for 6/11/16 visited the line with B.M. A.C.	
	10/11		As for 9/11/16 Repairs to SIEGE FARM. Stables dug out for O.C. FRONT LINE A.C.	
	11/11		As for 10/11/16 A.C. D Coy 11 N.NANTS. posted from 47 Bde.	
	12/11		As for 11/11/16 A.C.	
	13/11		As for 12/11/16 A.C.	

WAR DIARY
or
INTELLIGENCE SUMMARY.
(Erase heading not required.)

Army Form C. 2118.

156 FA G.B.R

Place	Date 1916	Hour	Summary of Events and Information	Remarks and references to Appendices
	14/11		As for 13/11/16 Q.C.	
	15/11		As for 14/11/16 Q.C.	
	16/11		As for 15/11/16 Q.C.	
	17/11		As for 16/11/16 Q.C.	
	18/11		Started Charge at Lantern for 47 Bde. As for 17/11/16 Q.C.	
	19/11		As for 18/11/16 Q.C.	
	20/11		Started work on O.P. - VAN KEEP Q.C.	
	21/11		As for 20/11/16 Q.C.	
	22/11		As for 21/11/16 Q.C.	
	23/11		Sent platelayers to work on Tramway. Q.C. Revised working party table with B.M. Q.C.	
	24/11		As for 24/11/16 Q.C.	
	25/11		As for 25/11/16 Q.C. O.C. returns to Company.	
	27/11		Work as on 26.11.16 am	
	28/11		As for 27.11.16 pm	
	29/11		As for 28.11.16 pm	
	30/11		As for 29.11.16 pm	

R.M.W. Meurier
Captain
O.C. 156 Fd Ry

WAR DIARY FOR MONTH OF DECEMBER, 1915.

VOLUME ~~B~~

156th Field Coy R.E.

Vol 13

WAR DIARY

INTELLIGENCE SUMMARY

Army Form C. 2118.

December 1916.

156 Field Coy. R.E.

Instructions regarding War Diaries and Intelligence Summaries are contained in F. S. Regs., Part II. and the Staff Manual respectively. Title pages will be prepared in manuscript.

Place	Date	Hour	Summary of Events and Information	Remarks and references to Appendices
PIONEER FM	1.12.16		Company at work repairing and rebuilding front line, making new supports line, COBB TRENCH, artillery O.P., HTM emplacement. Bn section putting R.M. to [?] for 1.12.16 R.M.	
"	2.12.16		Work as for 2.12.16. Ot. waited hours held by 109" BDE, 26 DIVN, until G. 150. Field Coy, and took over details of work. R.M.	
"	3.12.16			
"	4.12.16		Ot. waited down hours with Judion Officer, and overview blocks over LURGAN CAMP from 16 R.I.R.fk(P) R.M.	
"	5.12.16		Two sections moved to BUS FARM, and commenced work on front line TRAN system	
LURGAN CAMP	6.12.16		BROEK butter R.P. 47 INF. BDE in line R.M. Coy Hdqrs and one section moved to LURGAN CAMP, and took over camp from 16 R.I.Rifle (P). Work in line as on 5.12.16 R.M.	
"	7.12.16		Work as on 6.12.16 R.M.	
"	8.12.16		Work as on 7.12.16 R.M.	
"	9.12.16		Work as on 8.12.16 R.M.	
"	10.12.16		Work as on 9.12.16 R.M.	
"	11.12.16		Work as on 10.12.16 R.M.	

Army Form C. 2118.

WAR DIARY
or
INTELLIGENCE SUMMARY.
(Erase heading not required.)

157 Fd Coy R.E.

Place	Date	Hour	Summary of Events and Information	Remarks and references to Appendices
DRANOUTRE	12.12.16		Work on 11.12.16. RM	
"	13.12.16		do for 12.12.16 RM	
"	14.12.16		do for 13.12.16 RM	
"	15.12.16		do for 14.12.16 RM	
"	16.12.16		do for 15.12.16 RM	
"	17.12.16		Front line much damaged by enemy. Work on repairing, revetting, drawing front line again. 1 TM empl. and 1 Stokes empl. intact. Work on 2 Reune dug out and improving am dressing & accommodation for gunners & trench. Carrier started near R.E. Farm RM	
"	18.12.16		Work on 17.12.16 RM	
"	19.12.16		Work on 18.12.16 RM	
"	20.12.16		Work on 19.12.16 RM	
"	21.12.16		Work on 20.12.16 RM	
"	22.12.16		Work on 21.12.16 RM	
"	23.12.16		Work on 22.12.16 RM	
"	24.12.16		Work on 23.12.16 RM	
"	26.12.16		Holiday RM	

Army Form C. 2118.

WAR DIARY
~~INTELLIGENCE SUMMARY~~
156 FIELD COY R.E.
(Erase heading not required.)

Instructions regarding War Diaries and Intelligence Summaries are contained in F. S. Regs., Part II. and the Staff Manual respectively. Title pages will be prepared in manuscript.

Place	Date	Hour	Summary of Events and Information	Remarks and references to Appendices
DRANOUTRE	26.12.15		One Section working on hutting. Remainder to work maintaining and improving front line system & fireworks, making dugouts, Shelters & T.M. emplacements. Rm	
"	27.12.15		do for 26.12. Rm	
"	28.12		do for 27.12. Rm	
"	29.12		do for 28.12. Rm	
"	30.12		do for 29.12. Rm	
"	31.12		do for 30.12. Rm	

R.M.W. Marsden
Major RE
O.C. 156 Fd Coy RE.

WAR DIARY for month of JANUARY, 1917.

VOLUME 14

Royal Engineers 156th Field Company

Army Form C. 2118.

WAR DIARY
or
INTELLIGENCE SUMMARY.
(Erase heading not required.)

156 FIELD COY R.E.

Instructions regarding War Diaries and Intelligence Summaries are contained in F. S. Regs., Part II. and the Staff Manual respectively. Title pages will be prepared in manuscript.

Place	Date	Hour	Summary of Events and Information	Remarks and references to Appendices
DRANOUTRE	1.1.17		Coy at work on tunnels in SPANBROEK SECTOR: maintaining, repairing, draining front line system. Constructing dug out and T.M. empt. One section in hutting Rm.	
"	2.1.17		Do for 1.1.17 Rm	
"	3.1.17		Do for 2.1.17 Rm	
"	4.1.17		Do for 3.1.17 Rm	
"	5.1.17		Do for 4.1.17 Rm	
"	6.1.17		Do for 5.1.17 Rm	
"	7.1.17		Front line heavy STRETCHER LANE round damaged by hostile T.M's. R.E.F.P.M. demard. Work as for 6.1.17 Rm	
"	8.1.17		Work as for 7.1.17 Rm	
"	9.1.17		11th Hants take over work on HAPPIER MOMENTS G.C.	
"	10.1.17		Visited line with C.R.E. Work as for 9.1.17 G.C.	
"	11.1.17		Work as for 10.1.17 G.C.	
"	12.1.17		Front line in Right Subsection much damaged by hostile fire G.C. Work as for 12.1.17 G.C.	
"	13.1.17			
"	14.1.17		Attended Conference about Proposed field Work as for 13.1.17 G.C.	

Army Form C. 2118.

WAR DIARY
or
INTELLIGENCE SUMMARY.
(Erase heading not required.)

Instructions regarding War Diaries and Intelligence Summaries are contained in F. S. Regs., Part II. and the Staff Manual respectively. Title pages will be prepared in manuscript.

Place	Date	Hour	Summary of Events and Information	Remarks and references to Appendices
	15/1/17		3 Section at Work on FRONT LINE LONG LANE, ULSTER RD. DURHAM RD. and constructing dugouts, contain etc. 4.C	
	16-1-17		As for 15-1-17 4.C	
	17-1-17		As for 16-1-17 4.C	
	18-1-17		As for 17-1-17 4.C	
	19-1-17		As for 18-1-17	
	20-1-17		Visited HAPPIER MOMENTS and reported on scheme for stablichen communication f.b.	
	21/1/17		Work as on 20.1.17 RM	
	22-1-17		Visited HAPPIER MOMENTS and arranged for R.E. supervision and assistance between 15 N Hank (P) on this work. RM	
	23·1·17		Work as 22.1.17. RM	
	24·1·17		Work as on 23.1.17 RM	
	25·1·17		Work as on 24.1.17 RM	
	26·1·17		Work as on 25.1.17 RM	
	27·1·17		Work as on 26.1.17 RM	
	28·1·17		Work as on 27.1.17 RM	

WAR DIARY
INTELLIGENCE SUMMARY.
(Erase heading not required.)

Army Form C. 2118.

Place	Date	Hour	Summary of Events and Information	Remarks and references to Appendices
DRANOUTRE	29.11.17		16 Divn. Front reorganised into 2 Bde front. 47 INFBDE to take right section from DURHAM ROAD to BROADWAY, 48 to BROADWAY – VIERSTRAAT – WYTSCHAETE ROAD. 156 Fd.G.B. remain working in front area, Bty.	
	30.11.17		Work as usual. Rm	
	31.11.17		As for 30.11.17. Rm	

R.M.W. Marten
Major RE
OC 156 Fd. G. R.E.

31/11/17

WAR DIARY.

FOR MONTH OF FEBRUARY, 1917.

VOLUME 15

UNIT:- 156th Field Coy R.E.

Army Form C. 2118.

WAR DIARY
~~INTELLIGENCE SUMMARY~~
(Erase heading not required.)

156 Field Coy R.E.   Feb 1917

Instructions regarding War Diaries and Intelligence Summaries are contained in F.S. Regs., Part II. and the Staff Manual respectively. Title pages will be prepared in manuscript.

Place	Date	Hour	Summary of Events and Information	Remarks and references to Appendices
DRANOUTRE	1.2.17		Company at work on right sub section SPANBROEK SECTOR, 47 INF.BDE. in line. Work on maintenance and improvement of front line system of trenches. One section putting water	
	2.2.17		CRE. Work delayed by hard frost. RM	
	3.2.17		do for 1.2.17 RM	
	4.2.17		do for 2.2.17 RM	
	5.2.17		do for 3.2.17 RM	
	6.2.17		do for 4.2.17 RM	
	7.2.17		49 INF BDE relieved 47 INF BDE RM	
	8.2.17		Wrote on 1.2.17 RM	
	9.2.17		do for 7.2.17 RM	
	10.2.17		do for 8.2.17 RM	
	11.2.17		do for 9.2.17 RM	
	12.2.17		No 1 Section Bus Fm K DE 2 on for putting. No 3 Section DE 2 on K LURGAN RM	
	13.2.17		No 3 Section LURGAN CAMP to Bus Fm for work in Left of RE Subsection. No 2 Section LURGAN CAMP from BUS F.M for work on track to forward and L of pt 4 works. Works as usual RM	

WAR DIARY
INTELLIGENCE SUMMARY

156 Fd Co RE

Feb 1917

Army Form C. 2118.

Place	Date	Hour	Summary of Events and Information	Remarks and references to Appendices
DRANOUTRE	14.2.17		49 INF BDE relieved 49 INF BDE in SPANBROEK Sector. Work as usual. RM	
"	15.2.17		As for 14.2.17. RM	
"	16.2.17		As for 15.2.17 RM	
"	17.2.17		Thaw setting in. Work on CLOUTHER VALLEY and front line near STRETCHER LANE at a S.T.S.S. RM.	
"	18.2.17		As for 17.2.17. 11 HANTS (P) resumed work on HAPPIER MOMENTS and R.E. assistance. RM	
"	19.2.17/7.15am		1 N.C.O. & O.R. attempted raid on enemy lines unit 6 CONN. RANGERS. R.E. party carried explosives for demolition of T.M.s etc. Raid held up at enemy's wire. 6 to O.R. wounded. Normal work resumed at evening. RM.	
"	20.2.17		Work as usual. RM.	
"	21.2.17		As for 20.2.17 RM	
"	22.2.17		49 INF BDE relieved 49 INF BDE in SPANBROEK Sector. Work as usual RM	
"	23.2.17		Work as usual RM	
"	24.2.17		As for 23.2.17 RM	
"	25.2.17		No 2 Section moved to DE 2 on CAMP and took on hutting from No 1. No 1 Section moved	

Army Form C. 2118.

WAR DIARY
of
INTELLIGENCE SUMMARY.
(Erase heading not required.)

156 Field Coy R.E.   Feb. 1917

Place	Date	Hour	Summary of Events and Information	Remarks and references to Appendices
BRANOUTRE	26.2.16		to LURGAN CAMP. Work as usual Rm. No 1 Section moved KROS Fm and relieved No 4 Section in the line. No 4 Section to LURGAN CAMP	
	27.2.16		Work as usual Rm. As for 26.2.16 Rm	
"	28.2.16		As for 27.2.16 Rm	

R.M.W. Newsden
Major, R.E.
O.C. 156 Field Co. R.E.

28 FEB 1917

WAR DIARY
FOR MONTH OF MARCH, 1917.

VOLUME 16

UNIT:- 156th Field Company RE

Army Form C. 2118.

WAR DIARY
INTELLIGENCE SUMMARY.
(Erase heading not required.)

156 Field Co RE
March 1917

Place	Date	Hour	Summary of Events and Information	Remarks and references to Appendices
DRANOUTRE	1.3.17		Company at work in trenches SPANBROEK SECTOR. Division billeting. Transport and stables moved from DE ZON to LURGAN CAMP PM	
"	2.3.17		47 INF BDE relieved 49 INF BDE in SPANBROEK SECTOR. No evening working parties. PM	
"	3.3.17		Normal work PM	
"	4.3.17		As for 3.3.17 PM	
"	5.3.17		As for 4.3.17 PM	
"	6.3.17		As for 5.3.17 PM	
"	7.3.17		As for 6.3.17 PM	
"	8.3.17		Enemy bombardment during attack in VIERSTRAAT SECTOR damaged ULSTER RD, + LONG LANE and PICCADILLY PM	
"	9.3.17 A		Enemy attempted raid between DURHAM RD and KINGSWAY, but failed. In early morning. Work as usual PM	
"	10.3.17		No 2 Section rejoined Coy headquarters at LURGAN CAMP. No infantry working parties at night. Enemy attempted "Shuk-li" against Divisional attack PM	
"	11.3.17		O/C 121 Fd Cy RE (36 DIVN) visited LURGAN CAMP. Whole Coy work in	

WAR DIARY
INTELLIGENCE SUMMARY
(Erase heading not required.)

Army Form C. 2118.

March 1917

Place	Date	Hour	Summary of Events and Information	Remarks and references to Appendices
DRANOUTRE	12.3.17		SPANBROEK SECTOR. Officers and NCOs 121 F.Cy. visited BUS FM and finish. Work carried out on PICCADILLY Trenches and CLOUGHER VALLEY. RM	
"	13.3.17		Nonfunting parties with company at work on PICCADILLY trenches. RM. Sections relieved from BUS FM, LURGAN CAMP. BUS FM and work in SPAN BROEK. Julio Labor only 121 F.G.R.E. 1 officer sent to 237 FD Co RE (41 Divn) 15 week. Got work. RM	
"	14.3.17		O. visited work. 7 237 FD Co RE. RM	
"	15.3.17		Coy employed on improvement of BALDOYLE CAMP and walls. Movement to Hot Show area cancelled. RM	
"	16.3.17		One section employed on MILLE KRUISSE defences. Remainder at work CANADA CORNER and BALDOYLE CAMP. RM	
"	17.3.17		As for 16.3.17. RM	
BALDOYLE CAMP	16.3.17		Company moved to BALDOYLE CAMP. Handed over LURGAN CAMP to 121 FD Co RE (36 Divn). RM	
"	19.3.17		One section working on MILLE KRUISSE defences. Remainder employed training and work at BALDOYLE CAMP and CANADA CORNER. RM	
"	20.3.17		As for 19th. RM	

Army Form C. 2118.

WAR DIARY
INTELLIGENCE SUMMARY.
(Erase heading not required.)

156 FD. Co. R.E.

Instructions regarding War Diaries and Intelligence Summaries are contained in F.S. Regs., Part II. and the Staff Manual respectively. Title pages will be prepared in manuscript.

Place	Date	Hour	Summary of Events and Information	Remarks and references to Appendices
BADQUE CAMP	21.3.17		O.C visited Corps Reserve training area at FLETRE to arrange billets for company. PM	
FLETRE	22.3.17		Company moved by march route to FLETRE. PM	
"	23.3.17		Company training. PM	
"	24.3.17		As for 23.3.17 PM	
	25.3.17		As 24. 3.17 PM	
	26.3.17		As for 25. 3.17 A.C.	
	27.3.17		As for 26 - 3 -17 A.C.	
	28.3.17		As for 27. 3-17 O.C visited line with O.C. 155 Coy R.E. A.C.	
	29.3.17		As for 28 - 3-17 A.C.	
	30.3.17		Company moved by track parts to R.E. for relieving 155 Coy R.E. in line A.C.	
	31.3.17		At work on Front line VIERSTRAT Switch, CHINESE WALL. G.H.Q. line A.C.	

M. Carlyle CAPT. R.E.
for O.C. 156th FIELD CO. R.E.

31 MAR 1917

WAR DIARY FOR MONTH OF APRIL, 1917.

VOLUME:- 14

UNIT:- 156th Field Coy R.E.

Army Form C. 2118.

WAR DIARY
or
INTELLIGENCE SUMMARY.
(Erase heading not required.)

156 FD CO RE   April 1917.

Instructions regarding War Diaries and Intelligence
Summaries are contained in F. S. Regs., Part II.
and the Staff Manual respectively. Title pages
will be prepared in manuscript.

Place	Date	Hour	Summary of Events and Information	Remarks and references to Appendices
R.E.Fm. KEMMEL	1.4.17		Company at work on night extending VIERSTRAAT SECTOR. 47 INF. BDE. in line. Work	
	2.4.17		in front line. CHINESE WALL, VIERSTRAAT SWITCH, and G.H.Q. lines. R.W. Chaline construction	
	3.4.17		work on H.T.M. empl. in front of CHINESE WALL and on battery positions for R.F.A. statics. R.m.	
			At 7 pm 1.4.17 R.m.	
	4.4.17		At 7 pm 3.4. R.m.	
	5.4.17		Monday work as usual. R.	
		8.45 pm	2 N.C.O. 16 Sappers raided enemy trenches near MAEDEL STEDE Fm. and took 2 7 o from 6	
			R.I.Regt. Raid very successful. 21 prisoners taken 7 or not known up. R.m.	
	6.4.17		Normal work. R.m.	
	7.4.17		At 7 pm 6.4.17 R.m.	
	8.4.17		At 7 pm 7.4.17 R.m.	
	9.4.17		At 7 pm 8.4.17 R.m.	
	10.4.17		At 7 pm 9.4.17 R.m.	
	11.4.17		At 7 pm 10.4.17 R.m.	
	12.4.17		At 7 pm 11.4.17 R.m.	
	13.4.17		At 7 pm 12.4.17	

Army Form C. 2118.

WAR DIARY
or
INTELLIGENCE SUMMARY.
(Erase heading not required.)

156 F DC R.E. April 1917

Place	Date	Hour	Summary of Events and Information	Remarks and references to Appendices
REFM KEMMEL	14.4.17		As for 13.4.17	
	15.4.17		As for 14.4.17. No Infantry work. J.R.E. Fm. filled with one shell during afternoon. Bm.	
	16.4.17		At work on Breach in FRONT LINE S. of ASH LANE. Repairing BIRDCAGE, OAK TRENCH, ASH LANE. Building CHINESE WALL. Constructing H.T.M. on N.2, 5, 6, 7. Repairing VIERSTRAAT SWITCH. Building dugouts for M.O. Gym position. Q.C.	
"	17.4.17		(As for 16.4.17) Started work on New Coy H.Q. in S.P. 12. Q.C.	
	18.4.17		Work as for 17-4-17. Q.C.	
	19.4.17		48 Bde relieved 47 Iny Bde in FRONT LINE. Work as for 18-4-17. Q.C.	
	20.4.17		Work as for 19-4-17. Q.C.	
	21.4.17		Work as for 20-4-17. Q.C.	
	22.4.17		Work as for 21-4-17. Q.C.	
	23.4.17		Started work on H.T.M. emplacements other work as usual. Q.C.	
	24.4.17		Ordered by C.R.E. to report on Condition of FRONT LINE from Breach N. of ASH LANE to SNIPE CORNER. Work as for 22-4-17. Q.C.	
	25.4.17		Made a reconnaissance of FRONT LINE as ordered. Reported to C.R.E. that parapet was presumably good with exception of two points where it had sustained	

T2134. Wt. W708—776. 500000. 4/15. Sir J.C. & S.

Army Form C. 2118.

WAR DIARY
or
INTELLIGENCE SUMMARY.
(Erase heading not required.)

Instructions regarding War Diaries and Intelligence Summaries are contained in F. S. Regs., Part II. and the Staff Manual respectively. Title pages will be prepared in manuscript.

Place	Date	Hour	Summary of Events and Information	Remarks and references to Appendices
	26.4.17		direct hits with R.U.H. GARS. Expresses the opinion that with advent of dry weather lime might be reclaimed fairly easily. Conferred with Tunnelling Officer re diverting drainage of FRONT LINE ground entrance to Subway. 9.C. Confirms with Gnsat Ramsey reporting reclaiming of FRONT LINE. Started work on fire trench N. of ASH LANE. Other work as usual. 9.C.	
	27.4.17		As for 26.4.17 9.C.	
	28.4.17		As for 27.4.17 9.C.	
	29.4.17		As for 28.4.17 9.C.	
	30.4.17		156 field Coy take over VIERSTRAT SECTOR LEFT SUBSECTOR (from 156 Coy.) in addition to sector already held. Work on M.O. Gun emplacements handed over to 157 Coy R.E. 9.C.	

H. Cowley Capt. R.E.
for O.C. 138th FIELD CO R.E.

WAR DIARY:
------------oOo------------

VOLUME:- 18

FOR MONTH OF MAY, 1917.

UNIT:- 156th Labour Royal Engineers

Army Form C. 2118.

WAR DIARY
or
INTELLIGENCE SUMMARY.
(Erase heading not required.)

Instructions regarding War Diaries and Intelligence Summaries are contained in F. S. Regs., Part II. and Staff Manual respectively. Title pages will be prepared in manuscript.

1ST Fd Co RE
MAY 1917

Place	Date	Hour	Summary of Events and Information	Remarks and references to Appendices
R.E. FARM	1/5/17		Coy at work on repairing FRONT LINE, M.T.H. and M.T.M. gunplacements CHINESE WALL Machine Gun dugouts etc. CHINESE WALL hit by shell about 4.2" Calibre which passed thru 9ft thickness of stiff blue clay toppings, killing one man and wounding another in a dugout. R.M.	
	2/5/17		Work as for 1-5-17	y.l.
	3/5/17		as for 2-5-17	y.l.
	4/5/17		As for 3-5-17	y.l.
	5/5/17		As for 4-5-17	y.l.
	6/5/17		R.E. F-bd dump heavily shelled with 77 m.m shells setting fire to workshops and huts. Coy moved to DE ZON Camp. 4.2" C.B. believe to be responsible.	y.l.
DE ZON	7/5/17		Coy on work as for 6.5-17	y.l.
	8/5/17		As for 7-5-17 fitting cellars at R.E. farm with bunks etc. Q.L.	
BALMYLE	9/5/17		HQ and 2 Sections moved to BALDOYLE Camp. 1 Section moved to R.E. farm. H.Q. DE ZON Lewis K 81 Fd Co RE	

Army Form C. 2118.

WAR DIARY
or
INTELLIGENCE SUMMARY.
(Erase heading not required.)

Place	Date	Hour	Summary of Events and Information	Remarks and references to Appendices
BALDUKE	10.5.17		49 INF BDE relieved 47 INF BDE in VIERSTRAAT SECTOR. Coy moved to WOULDHAM CAMP (M 13.b.8.8.). BALDUKE CAMP handed to 82 F.G.Y.R. Rm.	
WOULDHAM CAMP	11.5.17		Normal work in the Camp being fixed. Or. arrived here with OR 1553 and 157 Fd Coy. and with a view to taking over. Rm.	
"	12.5.17		Work in line & round hill evening. Work in line taken over by 157 and 155 Fd Coys from evening 7.12.5.17. Coy moved to UPNOR CAMP, MONT RUGE. 3 officers, 100 OR. 76 CONNAUGHT RANGERS (47 INF BDE) permanently attached to 156 Fd Co for fatigue work and training Rm	
UPNOR CAMP	13.5.17		2 Section training on laying out & long point work, refreshing. 2 sections on "B" work for division. Rm.	
"	14.5.17		As on 13.5.17. Many Point out out and thing by 1 section with other infantry at night. Night wiring heavy carrying out Rm	
"	15.5.17		As for 14.5.17. Rm.	
"	16.5.17		Work started on artillery (R.F.A.) bridge in forward area. Other work e.t.c. 15.5.17. Rm	
	17.5.17		As for 16.5.17. Rm.	

Army Form C. 2118.

WAR DIARY
or
INTELLIGENCE SUMMARY.
(Erase heading not required.)

156 FD. COY. R.E.

Instructions regarding War Diaries and Intelligence Summaries are contained in F. S. Regs., Part II. and the Staff Manual respectively. Title pages will be prepared in manuscript.

Place	Date	Hour	Summary of Events and Information	Remarks and references to Appendices
HONOR CAMP	18.5.17		As for 17.5.17. Work carried on for new Field Artillery Group H.Q. at SIEGE FM RM. Work at SIEGE FM started. Also worked on for 18.5.17 RM.	
	19.5.17		As for 19.5.17 RM.	
	20.5.17		As for 20.5.17. RM Garrison shelter at SIEGE FM.	
	21.5.17		As for 21.5.17 RM	
	22.5.17			
	23.5.17		Arrangements made for finding men lent work &, and taking over forward work from 155 Fd RE RM.	
CHATHAM CAMP	24.5.17		Company H.Q. and 2 sections arrived, attacked infantry, moved to CHATHAM CAMP. 2 Parties moved to RE FM. Work on night siderton, WIERSTRAAT SECTOR, taken over from 155 Fd Coy RE. 4 S INF BDE in line. RM.	
	25.5.17		Work as on 24.5.17 but Company beginners in maintenance of two front system, completion of CHINESE WALL (PEKING), construction of medium and heavy hand mortar emplacements, getting up deep dugout, Infantile R.E.M. parties, alterations and deepening dugouts, packing up trench routes, also filling forward dumps. RM	
	26.5.17		Work as for 25.5.17 RM	
	27.5.17		Work on overland routes completed. No night work, parade every to read.	

WAR DIARY
or
INTELLIGENCE SUMMARY.

Army Form C. 2118.

Place	Date	Hour	Summary of Events and Information	Remarks and references to Appendices
CHATHAM CAMP	28.5.17		Relieved by 8th RDF wiring detachment of 155 F.D. Co. on enemy barricade. Rm. Party out on 26th. Nights not eventful with by enemy shelling. Rm.	
	29.5.17		Work normal Rm. Work on R.F.A. gun positions completed. Rm.	
	30.5.17		At 10.29 6.17 Rm. work on medium T.M. emplt. finished Rm.	
	31.5.17		Preparatory work for M.G. completed. New position of frontage to keep days out and filling forward dumps. Work during move much helped by fine weather. Rm.	

R.M.W. Marston
Major
O.C. 156 Fd. Co. R.E.

16/7

WAR DIARY.

FOR MONTH OF JUNE, 1917.

VOLUME :- 19

UNIT :- 156th Field Company R.E.

Army Form C. 2118.

Instructions regarding War Diaries and Intelligence Summaries are contained in F.S. Regs., Part II. and the Staff Manual respectively. Title pages will be prepared in manuscript.

WAR DIARY
or
INTELLIGENCE SUMMARY.

(Erase heading not required.)

156 Field Coy R.E.
June 1917

Place	Date	Hour	Summary of Events and Information	Remarks and references to Appendices
CHATHAM CAMP	1.6.17		Fittings for deep dugout completed. Water maintenance and filling advanced dumps carried on. RM. 47 INF BDE relieved 6.8.INF BDE in right section WIJTSCHAETE SECTOR.	
	2.6.17		Up to 16.17. RM.	
	3.6.17		TIT RANS DUMP Shelled (observed) destroyed - not repaired. Working party as yesterday commenced Pm.	
	4.6.17		Maintenance work and relieving dumps of stores 47 INF BDE confirmed. Pm.	
	5.6.17		Work as for 4.6.17. RM.	
	6.6.17		Orders received to move to assembly position. Final preparations for assault completed.	
		10.45 P.M.	Pack animals 20 in number, arrived at CHATHAM CAMP with to move up.	
		11 pm	10 shells near camp. 2 drivers wounded, 1 mule wounded, any time available. Pack mules	
			Collected and led up to position 9.5. Rm.	
	7.6.17	12.15 a.m.	Arrived at assembly position of attacked infantry arrived assembly position near IRISH HOUSE.	
		1.15 am	Co. arrived ROSS DUGOUT, headquarters of 47 INF BDE.	
		1.45 am	Remainder of company arrived at R.E. Farm and B.H.Q. 2nd Lines in vicinity	
		3.10 am	B. MINES EXPLODED, route enemy lines. Indian bombardment	

WAR DIARY
INTELLIGENCE SUMMARY
(Erase heading not required.)

Army Form C. 2118.

156 FD Co RE

Place	Date	Hour	Summary of Events and Information	Remarks and references to Appendices
		8.45 a.m.	enemy lines status accompanying our infantry advance. BLACK LINE reported captured. Sections sent out to work on consolidation and moving up stores in accordance with detailed instructions previously issued.	
		9 a.m.	O.C. proceeded to working party rendezvous saw parties off and issued material. Men visited work in hand on strong post, NAB POST, WOOD POST, CHURCH POST. Work proceeding well and stores coming to hand. Reconnaissance made for work in WYTSCHAETE and but sunken stone, arrow k ruined station, village.	
		5 p.m.	Work on NAB POST completed. Section returned to Coy H.Q. in STORK TRENCH (VIERSTRAAT SWITCH)	
		7.30 p.m.	Work on WOOD POST and CHURCH POST completed. Sections returned to STORK TRENCH. Hostile artillery fire from our side but not much reaction during day and night except in neighbourhood of WYTSCHAETE. Battle casualties 3 O.R. (R.E.) wounded. 3 other infantry wounded	
	8.6.17		Two sections and half infantry employed in moving stores from R.M. and getting stone for road metal. Putting into track in WYTSCHAETE. Party went	

Army Form C. 2118.

WAR DIARY
or
INTELLIGENCE SUMMARY.
(Erase heading not required.)

157 Fd Coy RE

Place	Date	Hour	Summary of Events and Information	Remarks and references to Appendices
			& clearing out what was found of spot where prisoner had expired. Water not found. PM	
	9.6.17	9 a.m	Company attended to CHATHAM CAMP, on 16 Gw from being taken over by 11 Div. Rest day. PM	
CHATHAM	10.6.17		1 Section at work in LOCRE laundry. Remainder attended Church Parade at which CRE was present PM	
CAMP LOCRE	11.6.17		Work on Division Laundry at LOCRE completed. Remainder company rest and training. PM	
	12.6.17		16 Div. moved to the ERRIS area. Fd Corps for work PM	
KEMMEL	13.6.17		Fd Coys proceed to camps on YORK RD (KEMMEL - VIERSTRAAT ROAD) for work on WYTSCHAETE RIDGE DEFENCES. Coy commander inspected line to prepare work PM	
	14.6.17		Company at work on WYTSCHAETE RIDGE DEFENCES from SOMER FM to NUTTER FARM. Construction of strong points, saps, firing lines, and joining up story fronts PM	
	15.6.17		As for 14.6.17 PM	
	16.6.17		Watermark by C.E. IX Corps unit acting C.E. Order received for 16" DIV to relieve 19 DIV in the line PM	

Army Form C. 2118.

WAR DIARY
or
INTELLIGENCE SUMMARY.
(Erase heading not required.)

156 FIELD COY R.E.

Instructions regarding War Diaries and Intelligence Summaries are contained in F. S. Regs., Part II. and the Staff Manual respectively. Title pages will be prepared in manuscript.

Place	Date	Hour	Summary of Events and Information	Remarks and references to Appendices
KEMMEL	17.6.17		Rest day. Orders received to hand over work to 82 F.D. COY R.E. of (19 DIV) and take over work from same company on going into line with 47 INF BDE. Orders cancelled on relief of 19 DIV by 16 DIV which followed. Ordered to move out of the line.	
OUTTERSTEENE	18.6.17		Company proceeded by march route to OUTTERSTEENE.	
	19.6.17		Company at OUTTERSTEENE. Strenth reports (30/M 89 OR. 6 C.R.) received to battalion.	
	20.6.17		Company proceeded by march route to EECKE.	
	21.6.17		Company proceeded by march route to POPERINGHE for work under C.E. XIX CORPS, FIFTH ARMY. Infantry Division proceeded to rest.	
POPERINGHE	22.6.17		Company fixing up camp at POPERINGHE. Officers arranging to take over work from XIX Corps H.Q.	
"	23.6		Work started on command H.E. 351 Siege for heavy batten at YPRES S. Work arranged for dug outs. Remainder of company training at close order drill and communication.	
"	24.6		Church Parade. Relieved by camp fatigues.	
"	25.6		Detachment returned from 351 Siege Battery owing to position being demolished by enemy fire. Work on expl. dug out stopped by enemy fire. Remainder of company.	

Army Form C. 2118.

WAR DIARY
or
INTELLIGENCE SUMMARY.
(Erase heading not required.)

Instructions regarding War Diaries and Intelligence Summaries are contained in F. S. Regs., Part II. and the Staff Manual respectively. Title pages will be prepared in manuscript.

Place	Date	Hour	Summary of Events and Information	Remarks and references to Appendices
POPERINGHE	25.6.17		Section close order drill and pontoon drill. RM	
	26.6		Lance bridge KRUISTRAAT - YPRES road. Apparel. Work on signal dug out KRUISTRAAT started. Remainder of company - having no infantry drill, parading Wootan huts Knotting, lashing, etc. RND work for 301 Siege Battery posted am.	
	27.6 28.6		As for 26.6. RM No 2 Section (2 Lt CULVER) and 7 Lt NORMAN detailed for Q work at 16 DIV HQ at No 1 Section (2 Lt NORMAN) detailed for Q work at 16 DIV HQ at KRUISTRAAT.	
	29.6		BEGGARS CASTELL. Remainder of company at work on signal dug out at KRUISTRAAT. Latter portion for 301 Siege Battery. Having it small and burying RM Company (less No 2 Section) working on signal dug out at KRUISTRAAT, burying position and ammunition dump for XIX Corps Heavy Artillery. RM	
	30.6		As for 29.6. RM	

R.M.W. Marshall
Major RE
O.C. 156 Fd Coy RE

30/6/17
1/7/17

WAR DIARY.

FOR MONTH OF JULY, 1917.

VOLUME :- 20

UNIT :- 156th Field Coy R/E

Army Form C. 2118.

WAR DIARY or INTELLIGENCE SUMMARY

(Erase heading not required.)

156 Field Coy RE
July 1917

Place	Date	Hour	Summary of Events and Information	Remarks and references to Appendices
POPERINGHE	1.7.17		Bne Section with 16 Div H.Q at ZEGGAR'S CAPPEL. Remainder of company at POTERINGHE. Work on ammunition dumps for XIX Corps H.A. RM	
	2.7.17		Work on battery positions for XIX Corps H.A. at YPRES. Work on signalling out at KRUISTRAAT. RM	
	3.7.17		As for 2.7.17 RM. Signal dug out damaged by enemy artillery. RM	
	4.7.17		As ret. on as for 3.7.17 RM	
	5.7.17		As for 4.7.17 RM	
	6.7.17		As for 5.7.17. 61, 58 and 70 H.A. groups visited, and sites reconnoitred near KAAIE for battery position for 81 Siege Battery. RM	
	7.7.17		Work as for 6.7.17 RM	
	8.7.17		No work. Inspection parade under 2IC. Church parade under 157 Fd C.E. Parade under 157 Field CRE for distribution of Parchment certificates awarded by G.O.C 16 Div for work in WYTSCHAETE operation. RM	
	9.7.17		Work as for 7.7.17 RM	
	10.7.17		As for 9.7.17 RM	
	11.7.17		OC visited work in YPRES area with CRE 16 Div. RM	

WAR DIARY or INTELLIGENCE SUMMARY

Army Form C. 2118.

156 FA Coy

Place	Date	Hour	Summary of Events and Information	Remarks and references to Appendices
POPERINGHE	12.7.17		Work as usual. PM SIC ration completed.	
"	13.7.17		Work on ammunition dump, well for 144 Heavy Battery, 303 Battery completed. PM	
"	14.7.17		Work on Signal Dugout (KRUISTRAAT) and 12 Heavy Battery. Dug for well commenced. PM	
"	15.7.17		Work on Signal Dugout (KRUISTRAAT) 12 Heavy Battery, two wells. Site selected, marked out and trellis commenced for BdO dugout for two signals Bde (Nissen Bow Hut). PM	
"	16.7.17		Work on Signal dug out (KRUISTRAAT), Repair dug out (KAAIE), 12 Heavy Battery, 3 wells and two BdO H.qrs. PM	
"	17.7.17		Work on 12 Heavy Battery continued. Work on repair of camouflage arms dump (DRILLERS) commenced. Otherwise a/fo 16.7.17. PM	
"	18.7.17		Work on Signal dug out (KRUISTRAAT) completed. Otherwise a/fo 18.7.17. PM	
"	19.7.17		Work on KAAIE dugout, DRILLERS Dump, 3 wells, and 2 Bde Hqrs completed. Orders received for company to move to WINNEZEELE No2 Area & reset. PM	
"	20.7.17		Company marched out WATOU to new area. NCO 2 OR detailed to VLAMERTINGHE for work on teacwavalin dug out 77 H.A. Group. PM	
WINNEZEELE	21.7.17		Company training in close order drill, musketry and Lewis section? from PM.	
"	22.7.17		Company inspection PM marching order PM. No 2 Section repaired PM road.	

WAR DIARY or INTELLIGENCE SUMMARY.

(Erase heading not required.)

Army Form C. 2118.

1st F.B. Coy R.E.

Place	Date	Hour	Summary of Events and Information	Remarks and references to Appendices
WINNEZEELE Area	22.7		In camps in ZEGGARS CAPEL area under 16 Div "Q". IN.C.O. and 2 O.R. rejoined from detachment at VLAMERTINGHE. R.M.	
"	23.7		Company employed on company drill, foolscray light trestle bridging and fork lashing exercises and practice demolitions R.M. Practice in laying sections of 9 ft. R.M.	
"	24.7		As for 23.7 R.M. 3 officers 100 O.R. 47 INF. BDE. attached for instruction and rest during afternoon R.M.	
"	25.7		Company proceeded and went under via WINNIZEELE and STEENVORDE to camp in WATOU No3 area. R.M.	
WATOU area	26.7		Company training in compass drive laying out tracks and mounting infantry on handles. R.M.	
"	27.7		Training on above. Also training pack team of 20 mules with infantry leaders R.M.	
"	28.7		As above. Also training infantry in rapid wiring and loading and carrying Yukon Packs. R.M.	
"	29.7		Rest day. Wet R.M.	
"	30.7		Orders received to move forward with 47 INF. BDE to BRANDHOEK area. Company proceeded by night march to new camp at BRANDHOEK	

Army Form C. 2118.

WAR DIARY
or
INTELLIGENCE SUMMARY.
(Erase heading not required.)

Instructions regarding War Diaries and Intelligence Summaries are contained in F. S. Regs., Part II. and the Staff Manual respectively. Title pages will be prepared in manuscript.

Place	Date	Hour	Summary of Events and Information	Remarks and references to Appendices
BRANDHOEK.	31.7.17		Company in camp between 155 and 157 Fd. Coys. RE	
		3.50 a.m.	Commencement of attack by Fifth Army. Coy in reserve to 16 Div, intend was in reserve in XIV Corps. Company standing by in reserve at Camp RN	
	1.8.17.			

R.M.W. Marsden
Major R.E.
OC 156 Fd Coy RE

WAR DIARY.

FOR MONTH OF AUGUST, 1917.

VOLUME 21

UNIT 156th Field Company R.E.

Army Form C. 2118.

WAR DIARY
or
INTELLIGENCE SUMMARY
(Erase heading not required.)

156 Fd Co R E

Instructions regarding War Diaries and Intelligence Summaries are contained in F. S. Regs., Part II. and the Staff Manual respectively. Title pages will be prepared in manuscript.

Place	Date	Hour	Summary of Events and Information	Remarks and references to Appendices
BRANDHOEK	1.8.17		Heavy rain all day. Company in camp under 2 hour notice. RM	
"	2.8.17		2 hour reduction removed. Work on camp improvement. Wet. RM	
"	3.8.17		As for 2.8.17 RM	
	4.8.17		Advance party took over camp at H.7.6.0.2. (Sheet 28) from 91 FD Co RE (15 Div). Company marched to new camp. One section employed on work at Div. HQ. Wet RM	
"	5.8.17		One section working at Div HQ. One section working at POTIJZE R.E. Dump. One section working at POTIJZE R.E. Dump. Or night YPRES PRISON & annexe with 113 F.A. about improvements at A.D.S. RM	
"	6.8.17		Work at Div HQ continued. Work at POTIJZE DUMP completed. Work at YPRES PRISON A.D.S. Work on road repairs and stable construction in Camp RM	
"	7.8.17		As for 6.8.17. Work commenced for ADS at POTIJZE and POTIJZE CHATEAU. For 113 Fd Amb RM	
"	6.8.17		Work as for 7.8.17 on PRISON, POTIJZE CHATEAU and POTIJZE ADS. Also construction of No 2 bridge over YPRES CANAL. Work on DHQ continued. RM	
"	9.8.17		As for 8.8.17. Also work on repair of bridge No 2 over YPRES moat. RM	

T/134. Wt. W708—776. 500000. 4/15. Sir J. C. & S.

WAR DIARY
or
INTELLIGENCE SUMMARY.
(Erase heading not required.)

Army Form C. 2118

Instructions regarding War Diaries and Intelligence Summaries are contained in F.S. Regs., Part II. and the Staff Manual respectively. Title pages will be prepared in manuscript.

Place	Date	Hour	Summary of Events and Information	Remarks and references to Appendices
BRAND HOEK	10.8		As for 9.8. Rm.	
"	11.8		Enemy aircraft bombed near camp 1 a.m. and 3 a.m. N.s. Casualties. Work as for 10.8. Rm	
"	12.8		Work on Bridge No.1 at YPRES finished. Bitumens as for 11.8. Rm	
"	13.8		Work on PRISON A.D.S. finished. 3 officers 90 O.R. 6 Connaught Rangers, and site from 7 Leinster Regt, sent to company for instruction in wiring Rm	
"	14.8		Work at POTIJZE new A.D.S. and at POTIJZE CHATEAU completed. Wiring parties being trained and engineered Rm	
"	15.8		Wiring parties further training. Wiring parties (Connaught and Leinster) with 12 R.E. and 7 McCULVER proceeded to position of assembly KRUISTRAAT, thence to IBEX and IBERIA trench. 1 off. 9 O.R. proceeded with lorry transport for water to ARMIN Hd. Qrs. erected section for dressing station, returning on completion. Remainder of company and details infantry bus transport moved to position of assembly near GOLDEN JAGER CMPT. Transport remained BRANDHOEK north West SHELLY Rm	
VLAMERTINGHE	16.8	4.45 a.m.	Attack by division on enemy position BREMEN REDOUBT - HILL 37. 1.55 Co. in reserve. Approx 11 Culver and 6 O.R. Loving parties returned to company, bringing	

Army Form C. 2118.

WAR DIARY
or
INTELLIGENCE SUMMARY.
(Erase heading not required.)

Instructions regarding War Diaries and Intelligence
Summaries are contained in F. S. Regs., Part II.
and the Staff Manual respectively. Title pages
will be prepared in manuscript.

Place	Date	Hour	Summary of Events and Information	Remarks and references to Appendices
VLAMERTINGHE	17.8.17		To infantry 2 party. Army organised to find lorries. Transport moved into your company. Completed intercommunication scheme day and night. 2 OR's killed & wounded. Company standing by at 1 hour notice. Camp shelled, bombs dropped in vicinity by E.A. at night. R.M.	
"	18.8.17		Advanced party sent to arrange billets at WATOU "B" area. Work handed over to 73 Fd Coy R.E. R.M.	
"	19.8.17		Cyclist and mounted parties proceeded by road to camp and billets at WATOU "B" area. Dismounted R.E. and attached infantry proceeded by train to POPERINGHE, thence by road to new camp. Attached infantry sent back to units. R.M.	
WATOU	20.8		Company proceeded by road route to EECKE to camp R.M.	
EECKE	21.8		Company proceeded to CAESTRE to entrain R.M.	
BAPAUME area	22.8		Company proceeded by train from CAESTRE to BAPAUME. Marched from BAPAUME to GOMIECOURT to camp. 16 Div transferred to VI Corps, Third Army. R.M.	
GOMIECOURT	23.8		Company resting and cleaning up. R.M.	
"	24.8		Company training in mine, gas, etc. R.M.	
"	25.8		O.C. visited O.C. 98 Fd Coy (21 Div) (V) to arrange taking over billets at ST. LEGER.	

Army Form C. 2118.

WAR DIARY
INTELLIGENCE SUMMARY
(Erase heading not required.)

Instructions regarding War Diaries and Intelligence Summaries are contained in F.S. Regs., Part II. and the Staff Manual respectively. Title pages will be prepared in manuscript.

Place	Date	Hour	Summary of Events and Information	Remarks and references to Appendices
GOMIECOURT	26.8		OC visited line with OC 12 K.R.R.C. to take over work in line. Rev. Church of England Church parade held under CRE at LONGEAST WOOD. Also 3 F.A. Coys present. After service, other parties on joined up. 16 Div Engrs inspected by G.O.C. 16 Div. Rev.	
ST. LEGER	27.8		Company proceeded to bivouac at ST. LEGER, for work in the neighbourhood of 16 Div front. 2 sections sent forward to dug outs in Quarry at J.14.c 3.1.B. V.19.a. Work on construction of bullet-aft ST. LEGER and improvement of Quarry. Heavy rain from 11 a.m. throughout the day. Rev.	
ST. LEGER	28.8		Relief of 21st Div by 16th Div completed. Work at outfall on PELICAN along front and deep dug out in front line. Work on billet improvement at ST. LEGER and Quarry. OC visited line with CRE, and proceeded to H.Q. 47 Inf. Bde afterwards to discuss work with G.O.C. Bde. Rev.	
	29.8		Work as for 28.8. Rev.	
	30.8		As for 29.8. Rev.	
	31.8		As for 30.8. Rev.	

A.M.W. Maunder
Major
31/8/17 O.C. 156 F.d Coy R.E.

T.2134. Wt. W708-776. 500000. 4/15. Sir J. C. & S.

WAR DIARY.

FOR MONTH OF SEPTEMBER, 1917.

VOLUME 22

UNIT:- 156th Fd Co. R.E.

156 Fld Coy RE

WAR DIARY

Army Form C. 2118.

September 1917

Place	Date	Hour	Summary of Events and Information	Remarks and references to Appendices
ST. LEGER	1.9.17		2 Sections working in front system of right sector of Divisional Front, on dug outs, foot-bridge improvements. One section working on dug out for forward section. One section working on hut billet of H.Q. O.C. attended conference of Section Commanders at which C.R.E. outlined proposals for work. RM	
"	2.9.17		O.C. and B.M. 47 INF BDE made thorough reconnaissance of front line to select an area for foot and defence of front line. RM. Lt ALLEN and detachment sent to work with 16 D.A. RM	
"	3.9.17		Division front re-adjusted. 47 INF BDE taking right portion and 48" taking lower portion on left. 47" L/Ls on the permanents, 48 and 49 to relieve each other. 156 Coy to stay with 47, 155 and 157 to divide remainder of front. O.C. visited trenches with G.O.C. 47 INF BDE and G.S.O.II 16 Div., and went further with Division of defence scheme. Lt GoE 62 Div fwd armement for defence. 163rd Inf Bde left No 62 Div left flank at BULLECOURT. RM	
	4.9.17		One section sent to HAMLIN COURT to billet with 157 F.A.Coy. and work on back area putting under C.R.E. One section working on Company H.Q. billet, stables, repairing and screening road from ST LEGER to MORT HOMME. 2 sections working on front system. RM	
	5.9.17		Work as for 4.9.17. Also work on retaining and screening road ST LEGER - HOMME MORT	RM

WAR DIARY
or
INTELLIGENCE SUMMARY

(Erase heading not required.)

Army Form C. 2118.

156 Field Coy R.E.

Place	Date	Hour	Summary of Events and Information	Remarks and references to Appendices
ST LEGER	6.9.17			
"	7.9.17		As for 6.9.17. R.M.	
"	8.9.17		As for 6.9.17. Also constructed weatherproof Coys O.P. for LOVAT'S SCOUTS R.M.	
"	9.9.17	9.20	O.C. inspected line with G.O.C. 47 INF BDE and reconnoitred line for support lines R.M.
		8a.m.	Test gas attack 9.30. Test continued R.M. 1/WINS gas projector, 1600 rounds, fired by 1 Special Company R.E. on selected point opposite front of company.	
		10.15pm	Gas alarm given, and company dressed and stood to. Heavy enemy gas shelling near CROSILLES and CHALK PIT found little.	
		11.30pm	Situation normal R.M. 1st summary of battle of GINCHY. R.M.	
	10.9.17		Work as usual. C.R.E. inspected company billets at ST. LEGER. R.M.	
	11.9.17		Work as usual. O.C. visited line with B.M. 47 INF BDE to settle further details of work. R.M.	
	12.9.17		Work as usual. R.M.	
	13.9.17		Heavy shelling by enemy in neighbourhood of STRAY SUPPORT. Normal work. R.M.	
	14.9.17		Normal work. Survey made of RAILWAY RESERVE for providing extra accommodation for infantry. Work on trenching new deep dug out in STRAY SUPPORT commenced. R.M.	
	15.9.17		Work on trenching new deep dug out in STRAY SUPPORT continued. NO 4 section relieve NO 1 section in right half of forward work of 47 INF BDE front. NO 1 section relieved.	

Army Form C. 2118.

WAR DIARY
or
INTELLIGENCE SUMMARY.
(Erase heading not required.)

156 F.D. Co. R.E.

Instructions regarding War Diaries and Intelligence Summaries are contained in F. S. Regs., Part II. and the Staff Manual respectively. Title pages will be prepared in manuscript.

Place	Date	Hour	Summary of Events and Information	Remarks and references to Appendices
ST. LEGER	15.9.17		Co Coy. H.Q. at ST. LEGER. No 2 Section relieved from detachment at HAMELIN COURT to ST. LEGER. Rm.	
"	16.9.17		Rest day. No 1 Section proceed to HAMELIN COURT for hutting. Rm	
"	17.9.17		Work as usual. Work on wooden accommodation for troops in RAILWAY RESERVE. Rm	
"	18.9.17		As for 17.9.17 Rm	
"	19.9.17		As for 18.9.17 Rm	
"	20.9.17		As for 19.9.17 Rm	
"	21.9.17		As for 20.9.17. MAJOR MARSDEN handing over to CAPTAIN SHELLY on being ordered to R.M.A WOOLWICH	
"	22.9.17		Company battled at ST LEGER. JS	
"	23.9.17		Work as usual. JS	
"	24.9.17		Work as usual. JS	
"	25.9.17		CAPT. L.S. HOLBROW R.E. (from R.E. Base Depot) arrived + took command of the Coy. Work as usual. JS	
"	26.9.17		Work as usual. JS	

Army Form C. 2118.

WAR DIARY
or
INTELLIGENCE SUMMARY.

(Erase heading not required.)

156 Field Coy R.E.

Instructions regarding War Diaries and Intelligence
Summaries are contained in F. S. Regs., Part II.
and the Staff Manual respectively. Title pages
will be prepared in manuscript.

Place	Date	Hour	Summary of Events and Information	Remarks and references to Appendices
ST. LEGER.	27/9/17		Work as usual. JS	
ST LEGER	28/9/17		Work as usual. ST LEGER - CROISILLES Road Shelled. JS	
"	29/9/17		Work as usual. No 1 Sec returned to ST LEGER from HAMELINCOURT. JS	
"	30/9/17		Rest Day. No 3 Sect returned to ST LEGER. Coy inspected by Brig Gen ERIGGS JS	
			G.O.C. of 4th INF BDE. 2.30pm. No 3 Sect went to HAMELINCOURT for huting JS	
			No 2 Sect went to CHALK PIT from ST LEGER for working hut JS	

James Skelly
Captain
O.C. 156 Field Coy R.E.

30/9/17

WAR DIARY

FOR MONTH OF OCTOBER, 1917.

UNIT 156th Field Coy RE.

VOLUME NUMBER 23

Army Form C. 2118.

WAR DIARY
or
INTELLIGENCE SUMMARY.
(Erase heading not required.)

156 Field Coy RE
Oct. 1917

Instructions regarding War Diaries and Intelligence Summaries are contained in F. S. Regs., Part II. and the Staff Manual respectively. Title pages will be prepared in manuscript.

Place	Date	Hour	Summary of Events and Information	Remarks and references to Appendices
ST LEGER	1/10/17		2 Sections living in CHALK PIT + working on trenches and new position Right Brigade Sector of Out. Post. One section at ST LEGER working on billets for Bde H.Q. etc. Support Batt. + for the Coy. JS	
"	2nd		Work as usual. Major T.L.S. HOLDEN Offg H.Q. + one to have been forward all day JS	
"	3rd		Work as usual. Leave allotted of 5 to 6 men per Coy to U.K. re-opened JS	
"	4th		Work as usual. JS	
"	5th		Work as usual. Major Holden returned to Coy H.Q. JS	
"	6th		Work as usual. JS	
"	7th		Work as usual. Officers N.C.O.'s + a man of Coy went to ERVILLERS to see lecture on "GERMAN LAND MINES and BOOBY TRAPS. JS	
"	8th		Work as usual. JS	
"	9th		Rest day for Coy. Lectures held at ST LEGER JS	
"	10"		Work as usual JS	
"	11st		Work as usual JS	
"	12nd		Work as usual JS	
"	13rd		No 3 Section left MAMETZ WOOD and arrived ST LEGER. Other sections worked as usual JS	

T2134. Wt. W708—776. 500000. 4/15. Sir J. C. & S.

WAR DIARY
INTELLIGENCE SUMMARY.
(Erase heading not required.)

Army Form C. 2118.

151 Fld Coy RE
October 1917

Place	Date	Hour	Summary of Events and Information	Remarks and references to Appendices
ST LEGER	14.		No 3 Sect returned to HAMELINCOURT for further work on huttings. No 1 Sect returned. No 4 Sect in the line. No 2 Sect came to ST LEGER. Weather usual.	
	15.		No 1, 2, 3, Section and one Party reconnoitred way in "No Mans Land" over which raiding party by No 2 were to go next night. The party were fired on when in German wire & withdrew. JS removal of Coy worked as usual.	
	16.		Major J.L.S. Brebner and 12 Officers & other ranks went and carried out 7 a LEINSTER Regt on TUNNEL TR No 1 BULLECOURT. Party entered enemy trench and made thorough examination of dug-outs & sub-sub etc. 3 prisoners captured by raiding party. 15 casualties among officers & other ranks arrived as usual JS	
	17.		Work as usual. JS	
	18.		Work as usual. JS	
			Work as usual. JS	
	19.		Work as usual. JS	
	20.		Work as usual. JS	
	21.		Work as usual	

Army Form C. 2118.

WAR DIARY
or
INTELLIGENCE SUMMARY.
(Erase heading not required.)

Instructions regarding War Diaries and Intelligence Summaries are contained in F.S. Regs., Part II. and the Staff Manual respectively. Title pages will be prepared in manuscript.

156 Fld Coy R.E.
October 1917

Place	Date	Hour	Summary of Events and Information	Remarks and references to Appendices
ST LEGER	22nd		Work as usual JS.	
do	23rd		Work as usual JS	
do	24th		Work as usual JS	
do	25th		Work as usual JS.	
do	26th		Work as usual JS	
do	27th		Gas bombardment of enemy's trenches opposite 17th INF BDE Sector. Work as usual JS.	
do	28th		Work as usual JS. No 3 Sect relieved No.3 Sect on hutting at HAMELINCOURT	
do	29th		Raid by 7th R.ININSK. Fus. on enemys front opposite 29it Bele Sector. Work as usual JS.	
do	30th		Work as usual JS	
do	31st		Work as usual JS.	

James Slelly
31/10/17.
Capt. RE
O.C. 156 Fld Coy RE.

WAR DIARY

FOR MONTH OF NOVEMBER, 1917.

VOLUME :- 24

UNIT :- 156th Field Coy R.E.

Army Form C. 2118.

WAR DIARY
INTELLIGENCE SUMMARY.
(Erase heading not required.)

156 Field Coy R.E.

November 1917

Instructions regarding War Diaries and Intelligence Summaries are contained in F. S. Regs., Part II. and the Staff Manual respectively. Title pages will be prepared in manuscript.

Place	Date	Hour	Summary of Events and Information	Remarks and references to Appendices
ST. LEGER	1st		2 Sections working on improving Front Line in 47th Bde Sector. One Section working on Batt H.Q. and shelters for support Coys on Railway Reserve. 2 C Coy H.Q., Bde H.Q., Bde H.Q. & Billets for advanced Sections. B Coy and Coy H.Q. One Section at Hanelmcourt on hutting. Rest day for Coy. No 2 Sect came to ST LEGER, No 3 Sect went to CHALK PIT.	
	2nd		Rest day for Coy.	
	3rd		Work as on 1st.	
	4th		Work as on 1st. 40 Men of 6th R. Irish Regt arrived for attachment to Coy for work and instruction in revving.	
	5th		Section worked as on 1st attached infantry improved their billets and made billets for another 30 men.	
	6th		Sections worked as on 1st. Training instruction of attd. infantry began. A further 30 men from 6th R. Irish Regt arrived.	
	7th		No 4 Sect. organised Coy from HAMELINCOURT. To 2 Sect and attd. Infantry practiced revving. Other sections worked as on 10th.	
	8th		Revving Signals organised each consists of 1 NCO. 3 RE & 6 Infantry, and practised in my b/l revving. No 1+3 Sects worked in line on revving.	

Army Form C. 2118.

WAR DIARY
or
INTELLIGENCE SUMMARY.
(Erase heading not required.)

13 E Fld Coy R.E.

November 1917

Place	Date	Hour	Summary of Events and Information	Remarks and references to Appendices
ST LEGER	9/11/17		Wiring squads training 1+3 Sections working in the line. JS	
	10/11/17		As for 9th JS	
	11/11/17		1+3 Sects as for 9th JS Wiring squads had rest day JS	
	12/11/17		As for 9th JS	
	13/11/17		As for 9th JS	
	14/11/17		Wiring squads practised at ERVILLERS laying ground in co-operation with Infantry who practised the attack. 1+3 Sections as for 9th JS	
	15/11/17		As for 12th JS	
	16/11/17		As for 10th JS	
	17/11/17		As for 14th JS	
	18/11/17		Nos 2+4 Sects relieved Nos 1+3 Sections in the line. Wiring party of 6th R. Irish Reg. & ST LEGER + 10th R/F advanced posts at TANK PIT. JS	
	19/11/17		Advanced Coy HQ established at TANK PIT. JS Nos 2+4 Sections worked in the line preparing for the attack on 20th. Nos 1+3 Sects rested. JS	
	20/11/17		Nos 2+4 Sects + wiring party of B 3rd Bn + 70 OR 6th R Irish Regt.	

Army Form C. 2118.

WAR DIARY
INTELLIGENCE SUMMARY
(Erase heading not required.)

157 Fld Coy R E

November 1917

Place	Date	Hour	Summary of Events and Information	Remarks and references to Appendices
ST LEGER	20/11/17		Took part in the attack on TUNNEL TRENCH N. of BULLECOURT, co-operating with 47th INF. BDE. The portion of TUNNEL TRENCH captured by the Brigade was wired. 2 bombing blocks were formed & 1 Comn. Trench marked out by these parties. The C.T. (BOW LANE) was partially dug. Nos 1 & 3 Sects moved up to CHALK PIT at 3.0 p.m. and worked on BOW LANE. Wiring parties completed wiring at night. CHALK PIT shelled at intervals throughout the day. JL	
	21/11/17		All sections together with wiring party worked on BOW LANE deepening and widening. CHALK PIT and ST LEGER shelled throughout the night. B 21/22 w JL.	
			No. 3 Sect. relieved No. 2 Sect. at CHALK PIT. No 4 Sect came to ST LEGER.	
			No 3 sect worked on BOW LANE.	
	29/11/17		Attack on MEBU "JOVE" by 7th LEINSTER REGT. A further 70 yds of TUNNEL TRENCH and Mebu JOVE captured. No 3 Section consolidated its position, wiring the flank and digging JOVE LANE. 2th Section revetted No1 sect held in readiness at ST LEGER, to move at a moment's notice in case of enemy withdrawal	

Army Form C. 2118.

WAR DIARY
or
INTELLIGENCE SUMMARY.
(Erase heading not required.)

152 Fld Cy R.E.

Title pages November 1917

Place	Date	Hour	Summary of Events and Information	Remarks and references to Appendices
ST. LEGER.	23/11/17		and advanced guard Jt.	
	24/11/17		No 3 Sect worked on BOW LANE & TUNNEL TR. No 2th Sect rested. No 1 Sect ready Some Jt	
	25/11/17		No 3 Sect worked on TUNNEL TR. other sections on Rest Jt.	
	26/11/17		No 2+4 Sects went to CHALK PIT & No 1 worked on TUNNEL TR. No 3 Sect came to ST LEGER.	
	27/11/17		No 1 Sect worked at ST LEGER. No 3rd Sect looked on Tunnel Tr. No 1 Sect went to CHALK PIT. No 3 Sect worked at ST LEGER. ST LEGER shelled at 11-0pm with 4.2"H	
	28/11/17		No 1+2 Sects working on consolidation of new positions including helios. O.G., G.O.G. & MAGOG. No 4 Sect at CHALK PIT, BDE H.Q., and at ST LEGER. No 4 Sect A Faring & wiring TUNNEL TR. No 3 Sect working at CHALK PIT. ST LEGER shelled at much lt with 8" shells Jt	
	29/11/17		No 1+2 Sects wiring & digging trenches in new positions around OG, GOG & MAGOG. No 4 Sect wiring & Faring TUNNEL TR. No 3 Sect working at ST LEGER. Jt	
	30/11/17		As for 29th CHALK PIT heavily shelled. Offs + 100 men (Infantry) arrived for attachment	

30/11/17 Jas Lelly
Capt. for O.C. 152 Fld Cy R.E.

WAR DIARY

FOR MONTH OF DECEMBER, 1917.

VOLUME :- 25

UNIT :- 156th Field Coy R.E.

Army Form C. 2118.

WAR DIARY

INTELLIGENCE SUMMARY.
(Erase heading not required.)

155 Fld Coy R.E.
DECEMBER 1917

Instructions regarding War Diaries and Intelligence Summaries are contained in F. S. Regs., Part II. and the Staff Manual respectively. Title pages will be prepared in manuscript.

Place	Date	Hour	Summary of Events and Information	Remarks and references to Appendices
ST LEGER	1st		Nos 1, 2 & 4 Sects worked on consolidation of TUNNEL TR. N. of BULLECOURT digging new trenches, 2 strong points, wiring and a Tramway. 100 attached Infantry worked with Nos 1 & 2 Sects.	
	2nd		No 3 Sect went to Clark Pt. & No 2 Sect came to ST LEGER. 100 attached Infantry returned to their unit to 16th Div.	
	3rd		relieved by 40th Div in sector E. of CROISILLES. 8 Field Coys of 16th Div worked in the line with 40th Div as the R.E. of 40th Div had not arrived. O.C. 229 Fd Coy R.E. arrived to ST LEGER in the evening. All sections returned. Coy packing up ready for moving.	
ST LEGER	4th		Coy left ST LEGER with orders to proceed to HAVRINCOURT. for work. Transport proceeded by road & dismounted men by Lorry. Messages received en route cancelling Hendecus orders. The Coy to rejoin the 47th Bde Group at BEAULENCOURT. O.C. 155 Coy & Coy camped for the night at BEAULENCOURT. O.C. 155 Coy	
BEAULENCOURT			remained at ST LEGER to hand over work to O.C. 269 Fld Coy R.E.	

Army Form C. 2118.

WAR DIARY
or
INTELLIGENCE SUMMARY.
(Erase heading not required.)

December 1917
152 Fld Coy R-E

Place	Date	Hour	Summary of Events and Information	Remarks and references to Appendices
BEAULENCOURT	5th		Coy billeted at BEAULENCOURT. O.C. 152 Coy Agoned from STIEGER	
"	6th		Coy proceeded to TINCOURT, by march route, moving out to 75th INF. BDE., from BEAULENCOURT, (distance 14½ miles). Arrived in TINCOURT at 5-0 pm & billeted for the night in the village	
TINCOURT	7th		Coy marched from TINCOURT to VILLIERS-FAUCON, and took over portion of the billets vacated by 1/23 Fld Coy R.E. at VILLIERS-FAUCON	
VILLIERS-FAUCON	8th		O.C. and officers of Coy went to RONSSOY to reconnoitre the village with a view to preparing a scheme for carrying out defence works of the village. Scheme of defence of RONSSOY prepared. Sections worked on improvements to billets &c	
"	9th		All sections went to RONSSOY & worked on the defences of the village, wiring, and digging posts &c	
"	10th		Sections worked as on 9th. Heavy shelling on RONSSOY – STEMILIE Rd. VILLIERS-FAUCON bombed by hostile aircraft. All personnel of Coy under orders to be ready to move at 2 hours notice	

Army Form C. 2118.

WAR DIARY
or
INTELLIGENCE SUMMARY.

(Erase heading not required.)

156 Fld Coy R.E.

December 1917

Instructions regarding War Diaries and Intelligence Summaries are contained in F. S. Regs., Part II. and the Staff Manual respectively. Title pages will be prepared in manuscript.

Place	Date	Hour	Summary of Events and Information	Remarks and references to Appendices
VILLERS FAUCON	11th		All sections worked on defences of RONSSOY A.	
"	12th		do for 11 hrs A.	
"	13th		do for 11 hrs A.	
"	14th		do for 11 hrs A.	
"	15th		do for 11 hrs A.	
"	16th		No 2 Sect. rested. Nos 1, 3 & 4 Sects worked on RONSSOY DEFENCES A.	
"	17th		No 1, 3 & 4 Sects rested. No 2 Sect. worked on defences of RONSSOY A.	
"	18th		Nos 1 & 2 Sects worked on RONSSOY defences. Nos 3 & 4 Sections worked on camps for Support Battalions near VILLERS FAUCON. A.	
"	19th		do for 18 hrs A.	
"	20th		do for 18 hrs A.	
"	21st		do for 18 hrs A.	
"	22nd		do for 18 hrs A.	
"	23rd		do for 18 hrs A.	

T2134. Wt. W708—776. 500000. 4/15. Sir J. C. & S.

WAR DIARY

December 1917 INTELLIGENCE SUMMARY.

157 Fld Coy R.E.

Place	Date	Hour	Summary of Events and Information	Remarks and references to Appendices
VILLERS-FAUCON	24th		Work as for 18th. Work on Lonssoy Defences handed over to 165 Fld Coy R.E. Orders recd. to move to Tincourt on 26th for rest & training.	
do	25th		Xmas Day. Coy rest Day. C.R.E. watched mens Xmas Dinner. Coy Concert held at 6-30 p.m.	
do	26th		Orders to proceed to Tincourt cancelled. Training of the Coy in Drill etc carried out.	
do	27th		Coy training.	
do	28th		As for 27th. O.C. 152 took over work in line from O.C. 157. Whole Coy paraded thro' gas testing Chamber & had bath in morning. Work in left Brigade area of Divl. Front taken over by 157 Coy from 151 Coy R.E. No 1 & 3 Sects went to advanced billets at Ronssoy. O.K.	
do	30th		No 1 & 3 Sects worked on trench work in line. No 4 Sect worked at Villers Faucon making frames for Shelters for the line. No 2 Section worked on new	

Army Form C. 2118.

WAR DIARY
INTELLIGENCE SUMMARY.

December 1917   1st Field Coy RE

(Erase heading not required.)

Place	Date	Hour	Summary of Events and Information	Remarks and references to Appendices
VILLERS – FAUCON	30th 31st		Coy H.Q. in ST. EMILIE. S. Foster 30th S.	
			1/1/18.	
			Ashley Capt. for OC 1st Field Coy RE	

Vol 26

WAR DIARY,

FOR MONTH OF JANUARY, 1918.

VOLUME :- 26

UNIT :- 156th Fd. Coy. R.E.

Army Form C. 2118.

WAR DIARY
or
INTELLIGENCE SUMMARY. (Erase heading not required.)

157 Fld Coy R.E. JAN. 1918.

Instructions regarding War Diaries and Intelligence Summaries are contained in F. S. Regs., Part II. and the Staff Manual respectively. Title pages will be prepared in manuscript.

Place	Date	Hour	Summary of Events and Information	Remarks and references to Appendices
VILLERS FAUCON	1st		Nos 1 & 3 Sections working in line erecting french shelters. Improving Batt. H.Q. etc. No 2 Sect working at ST.EMILIE 113 constructing new H.Coy H.Q. No 4 Sect working in + around VILLERS FAUCON making french shelters etc. J.S.	
do	2nd		as for 1st J.S.	
do	3rd		as for 1st J.S.	
do	4th		as for 1st J.S.	
do	5th		as for 1st J.S.	
do	6th		as for 1st J.S.	
do	7th		as for 1st J.S.	
do	8th		as for 1st J.S.	
do	9th		as for 1st J.S.	
do	10th		Nos 2 & 4 Sections moved up to RONSSOY to advanced billets and took over french work from Nos 1 & 3 Sects. Nos 1 & 3 Sec ts moved back to VILLERS FAUCON. J.S.	
do	11th		As for 10th. Orders received to hand over work here to 151 Coy R.E.	

Army Form C. 2118.

WAR DIARY
or
INTELLIGENCE SUMMARY.
(Erase heading not required.)

156 Fd. Coy. R.E.

JANUARY 1918

Place	Date	Hour	Summary of Events and Information	Remarks and references to Appendices
VILLERS FAUCON	12th		Nos. 2 & 4 Sections handed over to 57 Fd. Coy. R.E. & moved back to VILLERS FAUCON	
	13th		No. 1 Section working in St EMILIE constructing new Fd. Coys HQrs. Nos. 2 & 4 Sections wiring the Brown Line Defences. No. 3 Section working on PONSSOY Defences a.c.	
	14th		As for the 13th a.c.	
	15th		As for the 13th a.c.	
	16th		As for the 13th a.c.	
	17th		No. 1 Section relieved No. 3 Section. No. 3 Section working in area about VILLERS FAUCON. No. 1 & 4 Sections as for the 13th a.c.	
	18th		As for the 17th a.c.	
	19th		As for the 17th a.c.	
	20th		Nos. 2 & 3 Sections as for the 19th. Nos. 1 & 4 Sections had a holiday.	
	21st		As for the 14th a.c.	
	22nd		Nos. 1 & 3 Sections as for the 14th. Nos. 2 & 4 Sections moved up to PONSSOY to advanced billets and took over present tunnel work	

Army Form C. 2118.

WAR DIARY
or
INTELLIGENCE SUMMARY.
(Erase heading not required.)

156 Fd. Cy. R.E.

JANUARY 1918

Place	Date	Hour	Summary of Events and Information	Remarks and references to Appendices
MLF.R.S FAUCON	22nd (cont)		took over from the 1st Field Coy R.E. No.1 Mining Platoon (complete) & attached miners drawn from the 4yk/Argyll (Bn.) also moved up to forward billets in PONSSOY & took on dugouts & forward area. No 2 Mining Platoon made deep dugouts at rear area.	
	23rd		Coy H.Q. to 22nd	a.c.
	24th		As for 22nd	a.c.
	25th		As for 22nd	a.c.
	26th		As for 22nd	a.c.
	27th		As for 22nd	a.c.
	28th		As for 22nd	a.c.
	29th		As for 22nd	a.c.
	30th		As for 22nd	a.c.
	31st		As for 22nd	a.c.

Vol 27

WAR DIARY.

FOR MONTH OF FEBRUARY, 1918.

VOLUME :- 27

UNIT :- 156th Field Coy R.E.

Army Form C. 2118.

WAR DIARY
or
INTELLIGENCE SUMMARY.

156 Fld.Coy. R.E.

FEBRUARY 1918 (Erase heading not required.)

Place	Date	Hour	Summary of Events and Information	Remarks and references to Appendices
VILLERS FAUCON	1st		No 1 Section work'g in ST.EMILIE. Constructing new Coy. H.Q. No 2 & 4 Sections living in forward Lines at RONSSOY employed in forward area at work. No 3 Section work'g in & about VILLERS FAUCON. No 1 Mining Section living in forward lines in RONSSOY work'g on Deep dugouts in forward area mining. No 2 Platoon living in VILLERS FAUCON work'g in RONSSOY & ST.EMILIE on dugouts. R.E.	R.E.
	2nd		As for the 1st.	R.E.
	3rd		As for the 1st.	
	4th		No 1 & 3 Sections moved up to RONSSOY & took over the forward work from No 2 & No 4 Section. No 2 & 4 Sections moved back to VILLERS FAUCON. No 2 Section work'g in & about VILLERS FAUCON also assisting No 4 Section on new Coy HQ at ST.EMILIE. No 2 Mining Platoon took over work & Lines from No 1. Mining Platoon. No 1 Mining Platoon going back to VILLERS FAUCON to live & work'g in RONSSOY & ST.EMILIE on Deep dugouts. R.E.	
	5th		As for the 4th.	R.E.
	6th		As for the 4th.	R.E.
	7th		As for the 4th.	R.E.

Army Form C. 2118.

WAR DIARY
or
INTELLIGENCE SUMMARY.
(Erase heading not required.)

FEBRUARY 1918   1st Fld. Coy. R.E.

Instructions regarding War Diaries and Intelligence Summaries are contained in F.S. Regs., Part II. and the Staff Manual respectively. Title pages will be prepared in manuscript.

Place	Date	Hour	Summary of Events and Information	Remarks and references to Appendices
VILLERS FAUCON	8th		As for 4th ac	
	9th		As for 4th ac	
	10th		As for 4th ac	
	11th		As for 4th ac	
	12th		As for 4th ac	
	13th		No. 4 Section moved up to RONSSOY & took over "during" No. 1 Section, the work in the forward area. No. 1 Section moved back to VILLERS FAUCON to work on Coy's new H.Q. at ST EMILIE. The remainder of work as for the 4th a.c.	
	14th		No. 2 Section relieved from back work, and commenced training for future work. Remainder of work as for 13th ac.	
	15th		As for the 13th ac	
	16th		No. 2 Mining Section relieved No. 1 Section, the latter returning to VILLERS FAUCON to live ac	
	17th		As for the 13th ac.	
	18th		As for the 13th ac. 13th escape to Repas that the Coy. Hd. stables ic new H.Q. at ST EMILIE who 1st Repas Munster Fus; reaches the evening trenches this evening	
	19th			

Army Form C. 2118.

WAR DIARY
or
INTELLIGENCE SUMMARY.
(Erase heading not required.)

156 Fd. Coy. R.E.

FEBRUARY 1918

Place	Date	Hour	Summary of Events and Information	Remarks and references to Appendices
VILLERS FAUCON	19th Feb	11.0 a.m.	At 11.0 a.m. this Company sent over with them 1 Officer & from No. 2 Section & 5 O.R. from No. 3 Section armed with mobile charges for the purpose of destroying engagements & dugouts. The Sappers blew in the dugouts and assisted in bringing back prisoners. Nil Casualties.	
	20th		Relieved No. 3 Section by latter returning to the Company's new billets & St. EMILIE, the former later over the forward area work & billets in RONSSOY. No. 1 & Section or forward cont. Civil in RONSSOY. No. 2 & 3 Sections busy in St EMILIE works on Decauville & Bevil's R.C. dugouts. Mining features as for the 16th.	
ST. EMILIE	21st		As for the 20th	A C
	22nd		As for the 20th	A C
	23rd		As for the 20th	A C Coy H.Q. moved from VILLERS FAUCON to ST EMILIE
	24th		As for the 20th	A C
	25th		As for the 20th	A C
	26th		As for the 20th	

Army Form C. 2118.

WAR DIARY
of
INTELLIGENCE SUMMARY.
(Erase heading not required.)

Title pages 156 Fld Coy RE

FEBRUARY 1918.

Place	Date	Hour	Summary of Events and Information	Remarks and references to Appendices
ST. EMILIE	Feb 27		work. Co. for 20th & Order received to level over work in line & 97th Fld Coy R.E, 21st Div). OC. 97th Coy went over line with O.C. 156 Coy.	
do	28th		Order received to move to 76 O.C. 156 Coy. Preparing to move to rest area. Orders to proceed to rest area cancelled. Work continued as usual after receipt of cancelling order JK.	

J. Kelly Captn RE
for O.C. 156 Fld Coy RE

28/2/18.

16th Divisional Engineers

156th FIELD COMPANY R. E.

MARCH 1918

WAR DIARY
INTELLIGENCE SUMMARY.

152 Hallcroft March 1918

Place	Date	Hour	Summary of Events and Information	Remarks and references to Appendices
ST EMILIE	1st		No 2 Section took over work in front lines of Right Brigade sector from No 1st op. Sect. and moved up to forward billets in RONSSOY. No 1 Sect came back to ST EMILIE and took over work on RED LINE SUPPORT. No 4 Section went out to reserve at VILLERS - FAUCON. No 3 Section remained at ST EMILIE	
"	2nd		As for 1st.	
"	3rd		As for 2nd.	
"	4th		As for 1st.	
"	5th		As for 1st. VILLERS FAUCON lightly shelled.	
"	6th		As for 1st.	
"	7th		As for 1st. R.E. Forward billets at RONSSOY heavily shelled.	
"	8th		As for 1st	
"	9th		As for 1st.	
"	10th		157 Field Coy R.E. took over work in the line from 156 Coy. 156 Coy took over work on "BROWN LINE", + on ST EMILIE defences from 157 Coy. No 2 Sect moved from RONSSOY to VILLERS FAUCON. No 4 Section moved	

WAR DIARY
or
INTELLIGENCE SUMMARY

Army Form C. 2118.

156 Fld Coy RE

March 1918

Place	Date	Hour	Summary of Events and Information	Remarks and references to Appendices
ST. EMILIE	11th		from VILLERS FAUCON to ST EMILIE. No 1 Sect moved from ST EMILIE to VILLERS FAUCON.	
	12th		Coy had a rest day as all working parties were cancelled. Coy played 157 Coy at football. Nos 3 & 4 Sections working on BROWN line and BOIS SWITCH. No 2 Section working on ST EMILIE defences. Wiring new thing, etc. No 2 Section M.G. Emplacements and moving & building concrete M.G. Emplacements and moving &	
	13th		Do for 10th S	
	14th		Do for 10th S	
	15th		Worked for 10th S "Transport personnel + H.Q. details "stood to" in battle positions from 3.0 a.m. to 8.20 a.m. for defence owing to expected enemy attack. Sections & HQ details at ST EMILIE "stood to" in VILLERS. Sections from 5.0 am to 8.0 am. Sections worked as on 12th S	
	16th		Personnel at VILLERS FAUCON "stood to" from 5.0 a.m. to 8.0 a.m. Personnel at ST EMILIE "stood to" also. Sections worked as on 12th S	

WAR DIARY
INTELLIGENCE SUMMARY

Army Form C. 2118.

156. Fd Coy. RE

MARCH 1918

Place	Date	Hour	Summary of Events and Information	Remarks and references to Appendices
Villers Faucon	17th		Coy "Stood to" as on 16th.	
	18th		As for 17th N	
	19th		As for 17th N	
	20th		As for 17th N	
	21st		Coy looked as on 16th N	
			Enemy attack on 3rd - 5th Army fronts. Heavy bombardment of Coy Billets at STEMILIE and Coy Transport Lines at VILLERS FAUCON began at 4-45 a.m. including heavy gas shelling. Owing to this bombardment the Coy Transport Lines were evacuated at 9-30 a.m and all horses & wagons sent to LONGAVESNES. At 11-0am 2 sections at STEMILIE took up battle positions E.B. STEMILIE, & engaged enemy in the rifle + M.G fire during afternoon. Enemy broke thro an right flank & was driven to attacked by RE party led by C.S.M. + retired temporarily restored. At 7-0 pm Coy retired to Railway Cutting just E of VILLERS FAUCON where a line was established. The 2 sections at VILLERS FAUCON stood to all day in defence of the village till 7-0pm when they joined remainder of Coy in Railway Cutty E of VILLERS. Posts were established along in along STEMILIE road & manned all night N. Bombardment re-commenced at dawn. Enemy attacked at 6-0am. Garrison	
do	22nd			

Army Form C. 2118.

WAR DIARY
or
INTELLIGENCE SUMMARY.
(Erase heading not required.)

136 Fld Coy RE
MARCH 1918

Army Form C. 2118. Part II. Instructions regarding War Diaries and Intelligence Summaries are contained in F. S. Regs., Part II. and the Staff Manual respectively. Title pages will be prepared in manuscript.

Place	Date	Hour	Summary of Events and Information	Remarks and references to Appendices
VILLERS FAUCON and DOINGT			of BROWN LINE began to retire past the R.E. position at 8-30 am. The 2 sections R.E. with 11th HANTS holding posts along the road retired to Railway Cutting at 9-0 am & defended this position until units of 39th Div. retd. till 12-0 noon. The Coy retired fighting at 12 noon to GREEN LINE. 600 yds N.B. TINCOURT and later under orders of O.C. LINE to DOINGT. Transport moved at 11-0 am to DOINGT. Coy assembled at DOINGT and bivouacked.	MAP. FRANCE SHEET 62c. 1/40,000.
DOINGT BIACHES and CAPPY	23rd		Coy complete moved to BIACHES. Xing the PERONNE at 11-0 am. 3 hours rest at BIACHES. Coy moved at 3-30 pm to 1 mile NB HERBECOURT. (G. 30.d) & rested for 6 hrs. Coy moved at 9-0 pm to G. 28.a. & remained 1 hour. Coy moved at 11-30 pm. to 1 mile B CAPPY, and billeted in a barn.	
CAPPY	24th		Coy rested in billets remaining at & two motor lorries. At 6-0 pm all 4 sections in the 2 section transport moved to CHIPILLY 3/Brdge across River SOMME at SAILLY LAURETTE prepared for demolition. Remaining transport of Coy moved at 8-0 pm for PONT NOYELLES via BRAY & CORBIE.	MAP:— SHEET. "AMIENS" 17.
	25th		Coy at CHIPILLY. stood by for demolition of bridges. 3 sections moved at 6-0 pm to PROYART for defense of the village. 1 section remained	

T2134. Wt. W708—776. 500000. 4/15. Sir J. C. & S.

Army Form C. 2118.

WAR DIARY
or
INTELLIGENCE SUMMARY.
(Erase heading not required.)

MARCH 1918   156 Field Coy R.E.

MAP:- AMIENS SHEET 17

Place	Date	Hour	Summary of Events and Information	Remarks and references to Appendices
	26th		at CHIPILLY. Blow up bridges. Transport arrived at PONT NOYELLES at 6-30 am and bivouaced. Transport moved to WARFUSEE-ABANCOURT at 3-30 p.m. Section at CHIPILLY demolished 3 bridges over River SOMME and then joined 48th INF. BDE. Section at PROYART began to prepare a line of defence E of that village but owing to rapid enemy advance were ordered to discontinue work and take up defensive positions N. of PROYART facing N.E. At 7-0 pm Sect. received orders to withdraw under orders to a position on Chuignolles Road just S of MERICOURT facing E. At midnight 26/27th Section proceeded across tracks to MERICOURT to defend the South side of R. Somme at that point.	
	27th		At 5-45 a.m. Section at MERICOURT about 15 "a" part of above took part E of the village in touch with 49th INF BDE on right and 157 Fd Coy on left. Town heavily shelled. German attack began at 10-0 am + Section over bank took up position in MERICOURT lines of trenches in support. Section held on to the position till 3-0 pm + then retired with the general line of retirement. Section transport rejoined Coy Transport at WARFUSEE ABLAINCOURT. All Coy Transport	

T2134. Wt. W708—776. 500000. 4/15. Sir J. C. & S.

Army Form C. 2118.

WAR DIARY
or
INTELLIGENCE SUMMARY
(Erase heading not required.)

157 Fld Coy R.E.

MARCH 1916

Place	Date	Hour	Summary of Events and Information	Remarks and references to Appendices
	28th		moved to BLANGY-TRONVILLE and bivouacked. 1 & 2 Sections of Coy assembled at HAMEL and were ordered to remain there in support. Two sections with draw one details made 1st HALF moved into Front Line E of HAMEL. Transport pulled at 3-0pm in HAMEL ST.	
	29th		remained at BLANGY-TRONVILLE. O.C. Coy rallied at S. of HAMEL. Transport remained in support in sunken road just S. of HAMEL. Transport remained at BLANGY-TRONVILLE. 2 Section in Front Line. HAMEL shelled. 1 Section in support at HAMEL about to be sent to attack of regiment. Enemy opened heavy bombardment of Front line & supports at 8-0pm.	
	30th		attacked at 12-30. 156 & 157 Coys ordered to counter attack on portion of captured front line at 2-0pm. Counter attack across open took place & line re-established, touch being obtained with both flanks on retiring enemy engaged with rifle fire. Surplus transport moved to 1 mile E of FERRIERES. Remainder of transport stayed at BLANGY-TRONVILLE. Coy held portion of front line.	

Army Form C. 2118.

WAR DIARY
or
INTELLIGENCE SUMMARY. (Erase heading not required.)

156 Fd Cy RE

MARCH 1918

Place	Date	Hour	Summary of Events and Information	Remarks and references to Appendices
HAMEL	31st		500 yds. Coy in Front Line. F.J. HAMEL. To enemy attack on Coy. Surplus Transport & ammunition at FERRIERES. Remaining Transport moved to AUBIGNY. J. Stelly Capt RE o/c 156 Fd Cy RE 6/4/18.	

Vol 29

WAR DIARY

INTELLIGENCE SUMMARY

157 Fld. Coy. R.E.

APRIL 1918

Vol 29

Place	Date	Hour	Summary of Events and Information	Remarks and references to Appendices
HAMEL and AUBIGNY.	1st	3-0 am	157 Coy in Front Line E of HAMEL relieved by Cavalry Squadron (Dismounted) Coy marched back to SUNKEN RD near HAMEL and from there to AUBIGNY.	MAR:- AMIENS 17
AUBIGNY.		6-30 am	Coy arrived at AUBIGNY and rested there for the day.	
do	2nd		Coy rested at AUBIGNY. Spare transport moved to ABBEVILLE.	
	3rd		Coy moved to SALEUX. Transport proceeded by road. Dismounted men went by bus. Arrived at SALEUX at 8-0 pm & billeted.	
	4th		Transport moved at 7-0 am to ALLERY & billeted for the night. Dismounted men paraded at 1-30 pm for entraining at 4-0 pm but could not get on the train. Dismounted men remained at the STA at SALEUX till 12-0 m waiting for the train.	MAP:- ABBEVILLE Sheet 6.
	5th		Coy entrained at 12-30 am & train moved off at 2-30 am arriving at BLANGY at 7-0 am & detraining there. Dismounted men marched to ONICOURT. Transport moved from ALLERY to ONICOURT. Whole Coy billeted at ONICOURT.	MARS:- DIEPPE

WAR DIARY
INTELLIGENCE SUMMARY

Army Form C. 2118.

157 Fld Coy RE

APRIL 1916

Place	Date	Hour	Summary of Events and Information	Remarks and references to Appendices
ONICOURT (MAP:- ABBEVILLE SHEET)	6th		Coy in billets at ONICOURT refitting & cleaning up.	
	7th		As for 6th. Lt Culver & surplus Transport rejoined Coy.	
	8th		As for 6th. Capt C/B CRAMSDALE RE arrived & took command of the Coy.	
	9th		Coy inspected by CRE 16th Div. Refitting & cleaning carried out by Coy.	
	10		As for 6th.	
WOIREL	11th		As for 6th.	
(DIEPPE SHEET)	12th		Coy refitting & drilling in morning. Orders received at 2-30pm to move forthwith to WOIREL. Coy moved & billeted at WOIREL for the night.	
SEUX	13th		Coy marched from WOIREL to SEUX & Camped.	
(AMIENS SHEET)	14th		Work on CHR defence line taken over.	
	15th		Work on CHR Defence Line begun. Whole Coy worked on the line north of River + Indian Labour, doing tapeing out of trenches + wiring. Colonial labour did dig gang Jr.	
	16th		As for 15th Jr.	
	17th		As for 15th Jr.	
	18th		As for 15th Jr.	

WAR DIARY
or
INTELLIGENCE SUMMARY.
(Erase heading not required.)

Army Form C. 2118.

156 Field Coy RE

APRIL 1918

Place	Date	Hour	Summary of Events and Information	Remarks and references to Appendices
SEUX	19th		Work on G.H.Q Defence Line continued, wiring & digging.	MAP:- AMIENS Sh. 17.
"	20th		As for 19th	
"	21st		As for 19th	
"	22nd		As for 19th	
"	23rd		As for 19th	
"	24th		As for 19th	
"	25th		As for 19th	
"	26th		As for 19th	
"	27th		As for 19th	
"	28th		Whole Coy proceeded by march route to AILLY-SUR-SOMME arriving at 1.0 p.m. and entrained at 6.0 p.m. Train moved off at 10.0 pm via DOULLENS & ST POL to AIRE Area.	
"	29th		Ry Lt of 28/29 spent on train. Train arrived at THIENNES at 9.0 a.m. Coy detrained there and marched to PECQUERES billeting for the night.	MAP:- HAZEBROUCK Sh. 5.A
"	30th		Cox moved to work on defence line front E. of STEENBECQUE takenover. Billets at STEENBECQUE and arranged for work on defence line.	

Stoby Gatt
O.C. 156 Field Coy RE

1/5/18

Army Form C. 2118.

WAR DIARY
of
~~INTELLIGENCE SUMMARY.~~
(Erase heading not required.)

Instructions regarding War Diaries and Intelligence Summaries are contained in F.S. Regs., Part II. and the Staff Manual respectively. Title pages will be prepared in manuscript.

MAY 1918   156 F/O Coy R.E.   Vol. 30

Place	Date	Hour	Summary of Events and Information	Remarks and references to Appendices
STEENBECQUE	1st		Work on defence line at STEENBECQUE begun. 3 Coys Portugese Troops employed	MAP P.I.— HAZEBROUCK 5A.
do	2nd		by Coy on the defence line. No 1 Section moved to billets near STEENBECQUE STA. and carried out work on defended locality at LABAS. A	
do	3rd		As for 1st ft.	
do	4th		As for 1st ft.	
do	5th		As for 1st ft.	
do	6th		As for 1st ft. 2 Coys Infantry added to labour employed on work.	
do	7th		As for 1st ft.	
do	8th		As for 1st ft.	
do	9th		As for 1st ft.	
do	10th		As for 1st ft.	
do	11th		As for 1st ft.	
do	12th		As for 1st ft.	
do	13th		As for 1st ft.	

Army Form C. 2118.

WAR DIARY
or
INTELLIGENCE SUMMARY.
(Erase heading not required.)

156 Fld. Coy R.E.

May 1918

Place	Date	Hour	Summary of Events and Information	Remarks and references to Appendices
STEEN BECQUE H.Q.	14th		As for 1st	
do	15th		156 Fld Coy R.E. at Le HAUT, STEEN BECQUE STA and on Front Line taken over by 156 Coy. No 4 section with its transport moved to Le HAUT and took over billets there. No 3 Section moved to near STEENBECQUE STA. to billets. Coys work extended from C.24.b to I.16.a (a distance of 5,000 yds) and included Font-Surfport Reserve Lines & Defended Localities. Upon 1,500 men employed with the Coy on this work, 1000 being Portugese and 500 British Infantry	SHEET 36 N.W 20,000
	16th		As for 15th	
	17th		do	
	18th		do	
	19th		do	
	20th		Coy took part in Practice Training of Battle Positions at 9.0 am. Normal work was on 15th resumed at 11.0 am.	
	21st		As for 15th	
	22nd		As for 15th	

Army Form C. 2118.

WAR DIARY
or
INTELLIGENCE SUMMARY.
(Erase heading not required.)

Instructions regarding War Diaries and Intelligence Summaries are contained in F. S. Regs., Part II. and the Staff Manual respectively. Title pages will be prepared in manuscript.

Place	Date	Hour	Summary of Events and Information	Remarks and references to Appendices
STEENBECQUE	23rd		Work carried on on LILLERS - MORBECQUE Lnd Rd on 15 1st S.	
	24th		do for 23rd S.	
	25th		do for 23rd S.	
	26th		do for 23rd S.	
	27th		do for 23rd S.	
	28th		do for 23rd S.	
	29th		do for 23rd. STEENBECQUE bombed by E.A. at	
	30th		about 2 3rd STEEN BECQUE bombed by E.A.	
	31st		Portion of work of 157 Fd Coy R.E. Taken over by 156 Coy. 156 Coy work front extended from STEEN BECQUE STN. to Junction of CANAL DE LA NIEPPE and CANAL DE LALYS. SOUTH OF THIENNES. Work carried on as on 23rd	

Seely Capt.
for O.C. 156 Fd Coy R.E.
1/6/18

T2134. Wt. W708—776. 500000. 4/15. Sir J. C. & S.

WAR DIARY

INTELLIGENCE SUMMARY. 156 Fld Coy R.E.

June 1918.

Army Form C. 2118.

Vol 31

Place	Date	Hour	Summary of Events and Information	Remarks and references to Appendices
STEENBECQUE	1st		Work begun on new sector taken over from 157 Fld Coy R.E. Approx 1,100 Portuguese and 200 British employed with 156 Coy on work on KILLERS to BECQUE LINE. Work carried on in remainder of line J.S.	
	2nd		Coy rest day J.S.	
	3rd		Coy worked on KILLERS - MORBECQUE LINE soon 1st J.S.	
	4th		Look after 1st J.S	
	5th		do do 1st J.S	
	6th		do do 1st J.S	
	7th		do do 1st J.S	
	8th		do do 1st J.S	
	9th		No work (Sunday) J.S	
	10th		Coy looked after 1st J.S	
	11th		do do 1st J.S	
	12th		do do 1st J.S	
	13th		do do 1st J.S	
	14th		do do 1st J.S	

Army Form C. 2118.

WAR DIARY
or
INTELLIGENCE SUMMARY.
(Erase heading not required.)

156 FIELD COY R.E.

June 1918

Instructions regarding War Diaries and Intelligence Summaries are contained in F. S. Regs, Part II. and the Staff Manual respectively. Title pages will be prepared in manuscript.

Place	Date	Hour	Summary of Events and Information	Remarks and references to Appendices
STEENBECQUE	15th		Work on ~~MORBECQUE~~ — MORBECQUE — LILLERS LINE carried on as from 14th. St STEENBECQUE bghty. shelled N.	
do	16th		Coy. Rest Day. Usual weekly inspection carried out. N.	
do	17th		Work as for 15th N.	
do	18th		do for 17th N	
do	19th		do for 17th N	
do	20th		do do 17th N	
do	21st		Work as for 17th. Fever (so called Trench Fever) present amongst troops N.	
do	22nd		Work as for 17th N	
do	23rd		Coy Rest day. Usual weekly inspection carried out N.	
do	24th		Work as for 17th N	
do	25th		Work as for 17th N	
do	26th		Work as for 17th N	
do	27th		Work as for 17th N	
do	28th		Work on LILLERS - MORBECQUE LINE continued. on th Portuguese Troops. To Brtsh. Troops employed.	
do	29th		Work as for 28th N	
do	30th		do work close on trenches. Usual Coy weekly inspection carried out N	

1-7-18 Ulely Gerber
O.C. 156 FIELD COY R.E.

Army Form C. 2118.

WAR DIARY
or
INTELLIGENCE SUMMARY.
(Erase heading not required.)

156 FIELD COY. R.E.

JULY 1918

WO 95 32

Place	Date	Hour	Summary of Events and Information	Remarks and references to Appendices
STEENBECQUE	1st		Work for LILLERS—MORBECQUE line continued. M.L.	
do	2nd		As for 1st. M.L.	
do	3rd		As for 2nd. M.L.	
do	4th		Work continued with fatigue labourers. British labour no longer available. M.L.	
do	5th		As for 4th. M.L.	
do	6th		As for 4th. M.L.	
do	7th		Coy. rest day. Usual weekly inspection carried out. M.L.	
do	8th		As for 4th. M.L.	
do	9th		As for 4th. M.L.	
do	10th		As for 4th. M.L.	
do	11th		Coy came under C.R.E. "L" Sector for work. M.L.	
do	12th		As for 11th. M.L.	
do	13th		Do for 11th. M.L.	
do	14th		As for 4th. M.L.	
do	15th		Coy rest day. Usual weekly inspection carried out. M.L.	
do	16th		Work as for 4th. As for 11th.	

Army Form C. 2118.

WAR DIARY
INTELLIGENCE SUMMARY.
(Erase heading not required.)

JULY 1918   156 FLD COY RE

Place	Date	Hour	Summary of Events and Information	Remarks and references to Appendices
STEENBECQUE	17th		Work on LIERS-MORBECQUE Line carried away on 4th N. 22nd & 28th Portuguese. If Bates left this area and 12th & 14th Portuguese.	
			Of Batts arrived for work on alos line	
	18th		Work as for 17th J	
	19th		Work as for 17th J	
	20th		Work as for 17th J	
	21st		To work due on defences. Usual weekly inspection carried out	
	22nd		Work as for 21st J	
	23rd		Work as for " " J	
	24th		Work as for " " J	
	25th		Work as for " " J	
	26th		Work as for " " J	
	27th		Work as for " " J	
	28th		No work on defences. Usual weekly inspection carried out J	
	29th		Work continued as on 21st J	
	30th		Work as for 21st J	
	31st		Work as for 21st J	

Shelby Capt RE
For O.C. 156 Field Coy RE
31-7-18.

Army Form C. 2118.

WAR DIARY
INTELLIGENCE SUMMARY
(Erase heading not required)

AUGUST 1918
136 FIELD Cy. R.E.
W.R 33

Place	Date	Hour	Summary of Events and Information	Remarks and references to Appendices
STEENBECQUE	1st		Work on N. subsector of LILLERS-MORBECQUE LINE continued. Work consisted of completing breastworks, digging trenches, erection of wire-entanglements, construction of splinterproof & Reinforced Concrete shelters, and erection of open M.G. Emplacements for Batt. H.Q. of the Line. 1000 Portuguese employed.	
	2nd		Work as for 1st	
	3rd		Work as for 1st	
	4th		No work done by Portuguese. Coy parade + inspection carried out. 2000 new trenches sited & taped out ready for next day.	
	5th		Work on new trenches near STEENBECQUE begun.	
	6th		Work with Portuguese Labour as for 1st 159th, 712th & 733rd Labour Coys arrived in STEENBECQUE AREA for work with 136 Coy R.E.	
	7th		On LILLERS-MORBECQUE LINE A 3 Labour Coys (British) and 1000 Portuguese employed with the Coy on trenches, breastworks etc near STEENBECQUE	
	8th		MAJOR A.F. HUGHES arrived and took command of the Coy.	

L. Cork

Army Form C. 2118.

WAR DIARY
INTELLIGENCE SUMMARY
(Erase heading not required.)

156 FIELD COY RE

August 1918

Instructions regarding War Diaries and Intelligence Summaries are contained in F.S. Regs., Part II. and the Staff Manual respectively. Title pages will be prepared in manuscript.

Place	Date	Hour	Summary of Events and Information	Remarks and references to Appendices
STEENBECQUE	8th (con'd)		Work continued as on 7th	
"	9th		Work as on 7th. Officers of 135 A.T. Coy RE arrived to takeover work of Coy	
"	10th		Work as on 7th. Orders re handing over to 135 A.T. Coy RE cancelled	
"	11th		No work on defences. Coy parades & inspection carried out	
"			Orders received to prepare to move on 12th inst to CLÉTY	
"	12th		Coy paraded at 9.0 am in full marching order & left STEENBECQUE	MAP:— HAZEBROUCK 5.A.
CLÉTY			Coy arrived at CLÉTY at 1-5-0 pm and billeted. 549 Fld Coy RE arrived at STEENBECQUE at 1-0 pm. Billets and work handed over to 549 Coy by handing over party	
SENLECQUE	13th		Coy moved from CLÉTY to SENLECQUE by march route. Coy billeted at SENLECQUE. Handing over to 549 Coy completed and handing over party rejoined Coy at SENLECQUE	MAP:— CALAIS.13.
LACRES	14th		Coy moved to LACRES. Dismounted men went by Lorry transport by road. Coy billeted at LACRES and rejoined 16th Div.	
do	15th		Coy employed on cleaning equipment etc & fixing up billets	
do	16th		As for 15th	

WAR DIARY
INTELLIGENCE SUMMARY.
(Erase heading not required.)

Army Form C. 2118.

Place	Date	Hour	Summary of Events and Information	Remarks and references to Appendices
LACRES	17th 18th		Coy inspected by CRE. 16th Div. y. Transport of Coy moved with transport of 47 Inf. Bde from LACRES to QUILLEN. Leaving Lacres at 3-30 p.m. & arriving in QUILLEN at 7.30 p.m. & billeting there. Dismounted men B Coy remained at LACRES. A.	
	19th	9 a.m.	Transport moved from QUILLEN at 7.30 a.m, halted 1½ hrs near ERICEUX and arrived at ANVIN at 5.0 p.m. & bivouaced. Dismounted men proceeded by bus from LACRES to SAILLY-LABOURSE and billeted there A. Cyclists moved from LACRES BONINH by road & billeted there A.	MAP HAZEBROUCK and LENS 11
	20th		Transport moved from ANVIN at 8.0 a.m, halted near PERNES for 1½ hrs and arrived at MAISNIL-LES-RUITZ at 5-0 p.m & bivouaced there. Cyclists moved by road to SAILLY-LABOURSE & joined (A Coy) Coy took over work and billets from 26th Field Coy RE (1st Div)	
Annequin	22nd		First entered to handed over country duty of Agnts. 2 bns today where on to Annequin & me to billets.	
	23rd		With as to yesterday.	W.A.

Army Form C. 2118.

WAR DIARY
or
INTELLIGENCE SUMMARY.
(Erase heading not required.)

Instructions regarding War Diaries and Intelligence Summaries are contained in F. S. Regs., Part II. and the Staff Manual respectively. Title pages will be prepared in manuscript.

Place	Date	Hour	Summary of Events and Information	Remarks and references to Appendices
Annequin	24th	8/8	Work started on new pipe line. Thieve hut as before.	Bell
	25th	8/8	Work as for yesterday	654
	26th	8/8	Work as before.	655
	27th		Work started in chimney town Alley Thieve hut as before.	
	28th		Work as of yesterday. A total of 3 platoons from 13th batch reported in 24th for being in trench. Coll	
	29th		Work as before.	
	30th		Work as before.	
	31st		Work started in Rly. Alley. Thieve hut as before. O.C. 156th Field Co R.E. went round line before going into rest.	Rest

R L Hughes .... Major, R. E.

O.C. 156th Field Co., R. E.

Army Form C. 2118.

WAR DIARY
or
INTELLIGENCE SUMMARY.
(Erase heading not required.)

156 Field Coy R.E.

Vol 34

Sept 1918

Place	Date	Hour	Summary of Events and Information	Remarks and references to Appendices
Sailly Labourse	1.9.18		Work as usual till 5 p.m. Company entrained at S. Hemard Siding from Annequin & Sailly-Labourse in packets 1 & 2 via starting at 5.35pm. All officers returned track sent unworkable in account of Joroville enemy withdrawal. The section moved to Mazinquart.	all
	2.9.18		Chiefly & Bastin area. 3/ICSM Christie apptd to the duty.	all
	3.9.18		The Horse Lines moved from to Mazinquart from Mazinquart Rue 13. Work as usual. 12 men moved to Radinghem to find a Workingparty Camp.	all
	4.9.18		Work started on new lines but line late then was invested in front of Artillery abtd fighi. Work as before.	all
	5.9.18		Work as before, except started repairs shafts had to be moved Artillery bridge on the Cambrin - Le Bassée Rd.	all
	6.9.18		Transport Lines moved to new area at Meux-en-Mines. Work as usual.	
	7.9.18		Work as usual. Coy equipped with Lt. 14. Offer section + one RE & O.R. in H.Q.	
	8.9.18		Work as usual. Training of Lewis Gun teams begun.	
	9.9.18		Work as usual. Lewis Gun training carried on.	

Army Form C. 2118.

WAR DIARY
INTELLIGENCE SUMMARY

156 Field Coy RE

SEPTEMBER 1918

Place	Date	Hour	Summary of Events and Information	Remarks and references to Appendices
SAILLY-LA-BOURSE	10/9/18		Usual work carried on. L.C. Franey continued ⌀	
do	11/9/18		As for 10th ⌀	
do	12/9/18		As for 10th ⌀	
do	13/9/18		As for 10th ⌀ of ⌀ Glasgow withdrawn from bridge at L.21.a.0.8.	SHEET 44c.
do	14/9/18		One Section working on ROUTE 10 (A.20.a.5.2) erecting bridge + metalling track. Remainder as for 10th ⌀	
do	15/9/18		One Section continued ROUTE 10. One Section working on repairs to PEOS1 VERNELLES Road. One section working on pigeon camps near BERLIN ⌀ Reconnaissance made of locality of LES BRIQUES (A.21.R.) and of a Field to construction of a strong point there ⌀	SHEET 44a N.W. 1.
do	16/9/18		Work as for 15th ⌀	
do	17/9/18		2 Sections working on LES BRIQUES Defended Locality. One Coy ⌀ trench etc. One Section on ROUTE 10. One section on Camps near BARLIN ⌀	
do	18/9/18		2 Sections working on LES BRIQUES. Remainder on 17th ⌀	
do	19/9/18		As for 18th. 2 Platoons of Inf employed at LES BRIQUES ⌀	

Army Form C. 2118.

WAR DIARY
INTELLIGENCE SUMMARY.
(Erase heading not required.)

SEPTEMBER 1918 156 FIELD COY R.E.

Instructions regarding War Diaries and Intelligence Summaries are contained in F. S. Regs., Part II. and the Staff Manual respectively. Title pages will be prepared in manuscript.

Place	Date	Hour	Summary of Events and Information	Remarks and references to Appendices
SAILLY– LABOURSE	20th		do before	QM
	21st		do before	QM
	22nd		O.C. returned from leave. Work as before. Company relieved 135th Field Coy in former 2.Mils at Annequin. Capt Shelly went temporarily to command 155th Field Coy	QM
	23rd		R.E. Work reorganised. One company in two, one in support and one in reserve. Company employed Rections in Les Brignes, one in Cambrin & Avely, one on trenches & water supply	QM
	24th		Work as on 23rd. Lieut Culver attached to CRE's Office	QM
	25th		Work as before. New strong post at Rly village started	QM
	26th		do do before. Pt work started on new strong point	QM
	27th		do do before	QM
	28th		Work as before. Work on Railway # started at 10pm # and shelling.	QM
	29th		Work as before	QM
	30th		Work as before. Company strength 7 Officers 206 OR	QM

30.9.18

A.P.Hughes Major, R.E.
O.C. 156th Field Coy, R.E.

F.1 SR/7 Vol 35 (1)

Army Form C. 2118.

156th Field Company R.E.

WAR DIARY
or
INTELLIGENCE SUMMARY.
(Erase heading not required.)

October 1918

Place	Date	Hour	Summary of Events and Information	Remarks and references to Appendices
Annequin	1.10.18		Work was continued on the tramway up to Auchy les Brogues. Enzy point	All
	2.10.18		All ordinary work suspended on account of the famous withdrawal. Work on La Bassée train Rd. & on the La Bassée Douvrin Rd. at night. Reconnaissance parties out.	All
	3.10.18		Work continued on the 2 roads. Subaltern reconnaissance made	All
	4.10.18		Work started on a Tank Br. 172Am from Auchy & Bty. Berclau with 2 carpenters as working party.	All
	5.10.18		Work continued as yesterday.	
	6.10.18		As yesterday. Tank withdrawal as risked at.	
	7.10.18		Enzyneeried bridges under 20ft span. Br. carried by 2 men. Track continued	All
	8.10.18		Work as yesterday.	
	9.10.18		As before	
	10.10.18		Work started on platform gun-pits & one plank bridges and continued	
	11.10.18		Work as yesterday. 2 Sections moved a forward billets at Auchy	All
	12.10.18		& to forward billets under shelled a camouflage screen across Douvrin Brely Rd.	All
	13.10.18		Work as yesterday	
	14.10.18		Work as before	All
	15.10.18		Further German withdrawal. Lt. Hichon ETR up bridging par for 155th Field Coy Douvrin. 2 sent forward to Auchy. FW Br bridge over Aubigne & ditch to other side of Pt. Haute Deule. One other section	All

Army Form C. 2118.

WAR DIARY or INTELLIGENCE SUMMARY.

(Erase heading not required.)

156th Field Coy RE

October 1918

Place	Date	Hour	Summary of Events and Information	Remarks and references to Appendices
Annoeulin	16.10.18		3 Lieuts sent up to assist A.B. Alden Troolte bridge was erected at front of Column Rd a floating foot bridge at La Ferme. The troops have cleared from their bivys to Bavin. All sections remained in Billy Berclau that night.	all
Provin	17.10.18		Coy H.Q. moved from Annoeulin to Provin ↔ Sections from Billy Berclau to Provin with us on the Annoeulin – Carvin – Capelle – Gondecourt Rd. arriving at 1130 where present to put a long bridge across Haute Deule but started at 4.30 all material found in former Pioneer Park Bavrin. Sections started at 1800	all
Provin	18.10.18		Work started on bridge at 0830 3 sections + section from 5 155th Coy from 0900 Lift from 5 155th Coy from 1000 2 sections Work continued without interruption bridge completed at 2330.	all
Phelempin	19.10.18		One section moved early to Phelempin worked on various bridges Company moved later took on roads One section went to Canal + dismantled bridges slightly own.	all
"	20.10.18		Section general.	all
"	21.10.18		Work continued on roads between Phe Tourpin + Bavrin on section salt charging putting Phlempin stone. No 2 Section moved to Templeuve to start work on new	all
La Posterie	22.10.18		Exit bridge for the SCHELDT Company moved to La Posterie arriving at 1230	all
La Posterie	23.10.18		2 Sections employed on roads in Billy a Place Com'te 2 Sections working on bridge.	all

WAR DIARY or INTELLIGENCE SUMMARY.

Army Form C. 2118.

156th Field Company R.E.

October 1915.

Place	Date	Hour	Summary of Events and Information	Remarks and references to Appendices
La Panerie	24.10.15		Company employed on the main lorry route Templeuve - Genech - Cobrieux & on completing Stembeuroy & Florent the material for the trestle bridge.	AHH
"	25.10.15		As yesterday.	AHH
"	26.10.15		As yesterday.	AHH
"	27.10.15		As yesterday. A small bridge at #2. d near Templeuve opened and for heavy traffic.	AHH
"	28.10.15		Work as yesterday. A wood bridge at F8.c.3.1 repaired.	AHH
"	29.10.15		Work as before.	AHH
"	30.10.15		Work as before. Lorry party reduced to 60 O.R. C.M. billets gone into a new billet Carvent.	AHH
"	31.10.15		Work as before. Work started on roving bridge for road near Templeuve. Company strength 203 O.R. + 7 Officers	AHH

AHHughes, Major, R.E.
O.O. 156th Field Co., R.E.

Army Form C. 2118.

WAR DIARY or INTELLIGENCE SUMMARY.
(Erase heading not required.)

156th Field Coy RE

November 1918

VR 36

Place	Date	Hour	Summary of Events and Information	Remarks and references to Appendices
La Posterie	1.11.18		Work continued on roads & Trott bridge as last days of October.	all
Tantignies	2.11.18		Company moved to Tantignies arriving at 10 a.m. sites near the CRE's from 159th Coy & at work from 155th Fld. Coy RE. from 12 noon.	all
	3.11.18		Work consists of clearing entering Rumes. Bachy Rd. Rumes. Tournai Rd. & Florent-Rumes. Rd. about 100 civilians & 30 Infantry employed. Also population in Tantignies & Longue Sault. & continuation of site bridge	all
	4.11.18		Work as yesterday. CRS. returned. 2 floating bridges (except log flts made) sent of material. Two bridges completed by Cpl Sadler & Bruyelles at all wagons. Returned by 7.0.p.m.	all
	5.11.18			all
	6.11.18		A third bridge made at Bruyelles. Their work as before. A fourth bridge made at Bruyelles. Their work as before.	all
	7.11.18		CRS held conference at 155 Hqs & Coring Flamel. On earth bridge. but the made also experimented light boats. Work as before.	all
	8.11.18		News received about 9 am. that the Germans are withdrawing. All men recalled from with Carry B 10 lories all Rd's For an reported at 3 p.m. I started Sapr of to Antoing to sound Tunnel to see wether Company should to start Sof for bridge at dawn. Also the lory carry	all

D. D. & L., London, E.C.
(A8001) Wt. W1771/M2091 750x500 5/17 Sch. 52 Forms/C2118/14

Army Form C. 2118.

WAR DIARY
or
INTELLIGENCE SUMMARY.
(Erase heading not required.)

156th Field Company R.E.

November 1918

Place	Date	Hour	Summary of Events and Information	Remarks and references to Appendices
Colonne	9.11.18		I proceeded on the lorries with CSM & 4 OR to find canal being at 5.15 & reached the site after a little difficulty & commenced enquiry where best to left positions to send up the Company & attached Pioneers stores at once. Bridge commenced immediately in three sections about 10.30. All B. Pels sent forward recce site & company moved but entrained till 9 p.m. Great difficulty experienced in about of movement from nearing site & the cement.	all
"	10.11.18		The canal two 15ft deep in the centre & had a very difficult return. Work started at dawn all trestles launched by dark it was found necessary to night the troops with a girder overhang abt 4ft on the up stream side to counteract the current. Bridge then for lorries at midnight. Light lorry crossed at 2.45 next morning.	all
"	11.11.18		Work continued in round decking, handrails etc. & large practically complete except whilst foot paths on round end. News received that the armistice was signed at about 10.30.	all
"	12.11.18		Work continued abridge complete, when received at about 7 pm for move to ATH for park in ATH - TOURNAI Rd.	all

Army Form C. 2118.

WAR DIARY or INTELLIGENCE SUMMARY

(Erase heading not required.)

156th Field Company RE

(3)

November 1918

Place	Date	Hour	Summary of Events and Information	Remarks and references to Appendices
ATH	13.11.18		Company moved BATH complete about 22 miles being billeted at 7.45 arriving ATH at 4 pm. Billets in Rue du Mouton hostels reserved for self. There are 5 some from 295th R.C.Coy.	self
"	14.11.18		Just into town all OC Advancement 295* S returned took a lorry	self
"	15.11.18		Reveille built pigs. Took bus from 7.30 am to 5 pm	self
"	16.11.18		Work as yesterday. Arrangements made for the Company stays at 2 schools in ATH station	self
"	17.11.18		Work as before 3 lorries sent to Rocy filled helping material Work as before men's billets charged better billets 55th Div. These then continue	self
	18.11.18		Have Work as before Company bridge other	self
	19.11.18		Work as before. No action being take	self
	20.11.18		Work as before	self
	21.11.18		Work as before as each brigade at Lisle started also on each bridge a coal culvert	self
	22.11.18		Work as before. On civil foot bridge complete except abutment	self

Army Form C. 2118.

WAR DIARY
or
INTELLIGENCE SUMMARY.
(Erase heading not required.)

156th Field Company R.E.

November 1918

Place	Date	Hour	Summary of Events and Information	Remarks and references to Appendices
ATH	23.11.18		Work as before. Lt Clifford took on leave	all
	24.11.18		Work as before. 2 Field high men, 10 ordered commenced to clean front entr.	all
	25.11.18	0800	to enable us to execute work awaited for troops	
	26.11.18		Work as before.	
	27.11.18		Work as before. Materials arrived late at night for 2 trestle bridges over	all
	28.11.18		at ATH and at LIGNE	
	29.11.18		Work as before. Trestle bridge at ATH in position.	all
	30.11.18		Work as before. All trestle bridges completed ready for the roads	all
			Company strength 196 O.R. 7 Officers	

A.P. Hughes, Major, R.E.
O.C. 156th Field Co., R.E.

Army Form C. 2118.

WAR DIARY
or
INTELLIGENCE SUMMARY.
(Erase heading not required.)

156th Field Company R.E.

December 1918

Place	Date	Hour	Summary of Events and Information	Remarks and references to Appendices
ATH	1.12.18		Wk as before and 1st belt built	all
	2.12.18		A further bridge now saved. Culvert for siding commenced. All material ordered	
	3.12.18		Wk as before and started a Tek & Company Gym Hut	
	4.12.18		Wk as before	
	5.12.18		Wk as before	
	6.12.18		Further bridge completed. Capt Wilks sent out to replace Lieut Hulyer at Hym	all
	7.12.18		2nd belt no working. Company rest day	
	8.12.18		No work Company test day	
			Bridge at dyne repaired. New culvert placed on site & first picket up	all
	9.12.18		Wk as before. Preliminary culvert in yrd commenced. Tek completed	
	10.12.18		Wk as before Tek refixed	all
	11.12.18		Wk as before 1st horse trough finished	
	12.12.18		Wk as before	
	13.12.18		3 Plate girder bridge arrived and started on me	all
	14.12.18		Wk as before and machinery completed	all

Army Form C. 2118.

WAR DIARY
or
INTELLIGENCE SUMMARY.
(Erase heading not required.)

156th Field Company R.E.

December 1918

Place	Date	Hour	Summary of Events and Information	Remarks and references to Appendices
ATH	15.12.18		No work. Company Rest day	all
	16.12.18		Work as before Athfrous removed.	all
	17.12.18		Work commenced on 1st girder	all
	18.12.18		Work commenced on 2nd girder (30 mtrs span) bridge	all
	19.12.18		1st girder completed. Work commenced on the third bridge	all
	20.12.18		Work as before. Trestle bridge on Mons Line finished then work as	all
	21.12.18		before. Work continued on two girder bridges new aviation chemin at culvert.	all
	22.12.18		2nd Plate girder bridge completed	all
	23.12.18		3rd Plate girder bridge completed	all
	24.12.18		All Company clearing at culvert	all
	25.12.18		No work. Company dinner & concert	all
	26.12.18		No work.	all
	27.12.18		Clearing at culvert very heavy very little work	all
	28.12.18		As yesterday very heavy rain	all

WAR DIARY or INTELLIGENCE SUMMARY.

(Erase heading not required.)

158th Field Company RE

December 1918

Army Form C. 2118.

Instructions regarding War Diaries and Intelligence Summaries are contained in F. S. Regs., Part II. and the Staff Manual respectively. Title pages will be prepared in manuscript.

Place	Date	Hour	Summary of Events and Information	Remarks and references to Appendices
ATH	15.12.18		No work Company Rest day	all
	16.12.18		Work on bridge Aulnoye resumed	all
	17.12.18		Work commenced on 1st Plat girder	all
	18.12.18		Work commenced R.2nd Plat girder bridge (30 mtrs span) bridge	all
	19.12.18		1st Plat girder completed. R.2nd girder bridge the work as before	all
	20.12.18		Work as before. Work commenced on It Hirst bridge & on Trott bridge & Mons Lui. Finished steam work as before	all
	21.12.18		Work continued on the Plat girder bridges remaining clearing up as about	all
	22.12.18		2nd Plat girder bridge completed	all
	23.12.18		3rd Plat girder bridge completed	all
	24.12.18		All Company clearing up about	all
	25.12.18		No work Company dinner & concert	all
	26.12.18		No work	all
	27.12.18		Cleaning out culvert very heavy rain little work	all
	28.12.18		Do yesterday very heavy rain	all

Army Form C. 2118.

WAR DIARY
or
INTELLIGENCE SUMMARY.
(Erase heading not required.)

156th Field Company R E

December 1918.

(3)

Place	Date	Hour	Summary of Events and Information	Remarks and references to Appendices
ATH	29.12.18		Day. Heavy floods up clone and Offord in culvert & Dam them company employed on logs & Pile line of permanent water supply	nil
	30.12.18		Work as yesterday	
	31.12.18		Work as before by Offord & work started putting stringers across G.S. Pile Bridge. Company strength 7 Officers 201 O.R.	nil

A.P.Hughes. Major, R. E.
O.C. 156th Field Co., R. E.

1.1.19.

WAR DIARY

OF THE

156th (FIELD) COY. R.E.

From 1st January to 31st January 1919.

Army Form C. 2118.

WAR DIARY
or
INTELLIGENCE SUMMARY.
(Erase heading not required.)

156th Field Company RE

January 1916

Place	Date	Hour	Summary of Events and Information	Remarks and references to Appendices
ATH.	1.1.19		No work today. Off for the men	
	2.1.19		Work as before. Company employed on laying pipes for waterpipes & drinking 7/6 Pl in Sqn	all
			in ATH	
	3.1.19		Work as before yesterday.	
	4.1.19		Work as before. Pit huts erected	all
	5.1.19		No work	
	6.1.19		Work as before. Another Pit hut commenced near Ligne	all
	7.1.19		Work as before yesterday. Pit hut received & given 15th Div at 10th	all
	8.1.19		Work as for yesterday.	all
	9.1.19		No work for Company to have	all
Barry	10.1.19		Company marched past 8.45 am arrived new billets at Barry at 1300 hrs	all
Bez Velvain	11.1.19		Company left Barry at 900 arriving Bez Velvain at 1230	
Genech	12.1.19		Company left Bez Velvain at 900 arriving Genech at 12.45	
Martinsart	13.1.19		Company left Genech at 900 arriving Martinsart at 12.45	
"	14.1.19		Company making billets comfortable etc. CRE held chief conference at	all
"	15.1.19		1100 Company ——————— ——————— new billings etc Valmering	all

Army Form C. 2118.

WAR DIARY
or
INTELLIGENCE SUMMARY.
(Erase heading not required.)

Instructions regarding War Diaries and Intelligence
Summaries are contained in F. S. Regs., Part II.
and the Staff Manual respectively. Title pages
will be prepared in manuscript.

Place	Date	Hour	Summary of Events and Information	Remarks and references to Appendices
Montreuil	16.1.19		Stocktaking. Major Hughes left for tour in Paris. "Hi Chefs" entrant à Mons &	JW
	17.1.19		meet representatives D.M.O. in tank at Pont à Mons.	JW
	18.1.19		Stocktaking. Work continued on arrangements Pont à Mons.	JW
	19.1.19		Inspecting billets. Work at Pont & à Mons in afternoon. Half holiday	
	20.1.19		Sunday. Holiday.	JW
	21.1.19		Work on billets continued. Stocktaking. Offrs at Pont à Mons continued.	JW
	22.1.19		Work on above. Capt acted Off for excesses to Main Rose sports.	JW
			21 offr. nuntes left for Coucentration Camp Tournai for Demob Schools "Horandr"	JW
			on seven/period than in Pasta Conductor Offices learn a V.K. Repris	JW
	23.1.19		Work on an 21.1.19 above Major Hughes returned from Paris	JW
	24.1.19		Work on above.	JW
	25.1.19		Work on above. Work announces arrangements for Demob Recruiting. Major Hughes left to stay these in D.R.	JW
	26.1.19		Sunday. Part day holiday. Major Boneyence's party, any offr on return man Hughes.	JW
	27.1.19		Sunday. Temple outfield J.m./L.A.I.C. and continued to inspect kitchens and billets Pont à Mons.	
	28.1.19		Work on before. Path. Att. proceeded to Berres for much. Cal. returned on afternoon Offr.	JW
	29.1.19		16 other ranks left for Concentration Camp Tournai for Demob Schools. Majors Hughes left on party conduct office a few 14 days leave in U.K. Capt Webster and Capt Edwards is troop	
	30.1.19 31.1.19		10 ranks Concentration through Offices 4/5 M. Howards on before. Work on before. (4 offrs & 16 O.R. in Conc. Infant)	

{signature} Colonel B.E.
O.O. 156th Field Coy., B. E.

— CONFIDENTIAL —

WAR DIARY
of the
156th FIELD COY R.E.

from
1st FEBRUARY
to
31st FEBRUARY

Army Form C. 2118.

WAR DIARY
or
INTELLIGENCE SUMMARY.
(Erase heading not required.)

157 Field Coy. R.E.

February 1919

Instructions regarding War Diaries and Intelligence Summaries are contained in F. S. Regs., Part II. and the Staff Manual respectively. Title pages will be prepared in manuscript.

Place	Date	Hour	Summary of Events and Information	Remarks and references to Appendices
MARTIN SART	1/2/19		Work on repairs of baths demolished, bridge at COURRIERES commenced. 9 men Staff & dump for demolitions.	JW
do	2/2/19		Sunday – No work. A.R.H. McDaniel/Waters visits 3rd R.E.	JW
	3/2/19		Work at COURRIERES resumed, constructing coping. Party under Tindur-Randers went to 157 Field Coy. R.E.	JW
	4/2/19		Work as before	JW
	5/2/19		Work as before	JW
	6/2/19		Work as before	JW
	7/2/19		Work as before. 89 O.R.s parade leave ie/ demobilization "Lt. Warrey of 9 men went from Leave in U.K.	
	8/2/19		Half Holiday. Work in morning as before	JW
	9/2/19		Sunday. No work. 6 other ranks leave for demobilization	
	10/2/19		Work as on 8/2/19 7 other ranks leave for demobilization. Major G. H Byrnes again went from leave in U.K.	JW
	11/2/19		do do before. Capt. F. Webster ret'n leave	AM
	12/2/19		do do before Lieut Walsh.	AM
	13/2/19		do do before	AM
	14/2/19		do do before	AM
	15/2/19		do do before	AM Halfholiday

Army Form C. 2118.

WAR DIARY
or
INTELLIGENCE SUMMARY.
(Erase heading not required.)

156th Field Company R.E.   February 1919   (2)

Instructions regarding War Diaries and Intelligence Summaries are contained in F. S. Regs., Part II. and the Staff Manual respectively. Title pages will be prepared in manuscript.

Place	Date	Hour	Summary of Events and Information	Remarks and references to Appendices
Martinsart	16.2.19		Holiday. Whit Mon & Tues. B church Sunday	
	17.2.19		Thos robichon cone cut firm. no ink at Gorvins	
	18.2.19		As yesterday	
	19.2.19		Orders received to make reservoir at Berm. No lorries allowed	
	20.2.19		Work started at Berm. 15 men from Somonts in groups	
	21.2.19		Work as before. 7 men sent over Blois at Berm	
	22.2.19		Work as before	
	23.2.19		Sunday. No work.	
	24.2.19		Work as before. No men from Somonts	
	25.2.19		Work as before. 9 men from 155 Fd Camp Ktps in groups 10 men from London	
	26.2.19		Work as before.	
	27.2.19		Camp completed ready for rous	
	28.2.19		No work. 16th Dr reviewing khat.	

A.W.Hughes Major, R.E.
O.C. 156th Field Co., R.E.

Army Form C/2118

WAR DIARY
or
INTELLIGENCE SUMMARY.
(Erase heading not required.)

156th Field Company R.E.

Instructions regarding War Diaries and Intelligence
Summaries are contained in F. S. Regs., Part II.
and the Staff Manual respectively. Title pages
will be prepared in manuscript.

March 1919

Place	Date	Hour	Summary of Events and Information	Remarks and references to Appendices
MARTINSART	1.3.19		Work as before on bridge at Courriere	
"	2.3.19		Sunday. No work	
"	3.3.19		Work continued at Courriere	
"	4.3.19		Work as before. 21 animals sent to Tournai	
	5.3.19		Ditto as before.	
	6.3.19		Ditto as before.	
	7.3.19		Ditto as before.	
	8.3.19		Half day company fatigue	
	9.3.19		Sunday. No work	
	10.3.19		Work continued at Courriere	
	11.3.19		Do. for yesterday.	
	12.3.19		Do. for yesterday. 1 L.D. horse sent to 108th Bde. R.F.A.	
	13.3.19		Do. for yesterday. 1 L.D. " " " " 18 animals sent to	
			Mons. en. Pevele for ocl. 13 animals sent to No 4 Base remount depot.	
	14.3.19		Do. before.	
	15.3.19		Half day company fatigue	
	16.3.19		Sunday. Capt Webster left for Marchlechin R.E Field Coy. & Attrichee	
	17.3.19		Publication printed at Templeure Divisional Staff	

Army Form C. 2118.

WAR DIARY
or
INTELLIGENCE SUMMARY.
(Erase heading not required.)

156th Field Company RE (2)

March 1919.

Place	Date	Hour	Summary of Events and Information	Remarks and references to Appendices
Martinsart	18.3.19		Transport of Company stores moved to Brinvisad also Templeure also 3 men as guard.	
	19.3.19		1 G.S. wagon & Maxicart retained.	
	20.3.19		Move completed 7 horses sent to Rouen.	
	21.3.19		Sorting Company stores at Templeure.	
	22.3.19		Stores collected & also 200 Tram to come in. Last 8 mules have not been.	
	23.3.19		Half day. Company performed at Sunday. No work.	
	24.3.19		Bridge & Courrier completed	
	25.3.19		Lt Moray left for demobilisation	
	26.3.19		Repairs to billets	
	27.3.19		Washing and repairing vehicles at Templeure.	
	28.3.19		Company moved to Frotin. Move completed by 1300 hrs	
	29.3.19		10 men sent to help 157th G. section 2nd Lt Chope. Worrall & Semple posted to 157th Field Company R.E.	
	30.3.19		Cleaning up billets at Martinsart, & washing & drying wagons.	
	31.3.19		2 Tents erected at Templeure.	

A H Taylor Major, R. E.
O.C. 156th Field Co., R. E.

WAR DIARY.

156 Field Coy. R.E.

April 1919.

Army Form C. 2118.

WAR DIARY
or
INTELLIGENCE SUMMARY.
(Erase heading not required.)

Instructions regarding War Diaries and Intelligence Summaries are contained in F. S. Regs., Part II. and the Staff Manual respectively. Title pages will be prepared in manuscript.

56th Field Cy RE.   April 1919.   (1)

Place	Date	Hour	Summary of Events and Information	Remarks and references to Appendices
FRETTN	1.4.19		Chang began at Tenghure	
	2.4.19		as yesterday	
	3.4.19		as before	
	4.4.19		as yesterday	
	5.4.19		as before	
	6.4.19		Sunday no work	AM
	7.4.19		as before	
	8.4.19		as before	
	9.4.19		as before	
	10.4.19		as yesterday	
	11.4.19		as yesterday	
	12.4.19		as before	
	13.4.19		Sunday no work	
	14.4.19		Camp fatigues	AM
	15.4.19		as yesterday	
	16.4.19		as yesterday	
	17.4.19		as yesterday	
	18.4.19		as yesterday	
	19.4.19		as yesterday	
	20.4.19		No work	
	21.4.19		No work	

Army Form C. 2118.

WAR DIARY
or
INTELLIGENCE SUMMARY.
(Erase heading not required.)

PAGE 2   APRIL 1919

Ref. Maps 36
FRANCE 1/40,000

Place	Date	Hour	Summary of Events and Information	Remarks and references to Appendices
FRETIN X 28 b.5-9 FACTORY	22	09.30	Parade for work in Camp. One O.R demobilised 21/4/19.	—
"	23	09.30	" Major Hugh proceeds to U.K. on 8 day leave	—
"	23	09.30	Hand Company over to 2 Lt Broom	—
"	24	09.30	Work as before	—
"	25	09.30	" 1 O.R demobilised (Repat.)	—
"	26	09.30	" 10 O.R to BRUSSELS by lorry for 3 days leave.	—
"	27	09.30	"	—
"	28	09.30	" 1 O.R demobilised (Repat.)	—
"	29	09.30	" 1 O.R to U.K. on 14 days leave	—
"	30	09.30	" 2 Lt BROOM hand Company over to Capt. H.F. McKeen R.E. and proceeds to U.K. WINCHESTER for repatriation. Strength of Coy. Officers 1 on leave to U.K. O.R 45 of which 18 are on detached	—

Wollom Major R.E.

A/O.C. 156th Field Coy. R.E.

156TH FIELD COMPANY, R.E.
No. ....
Date 1/5/19

WAR DIARY
156 FIELD COY. R.E.

MAY. 1919.

CADRE

WAR DIARY

INTELLIGENCE SUMMARY.

MAY 1919   PAGE I   156 Field Coy R.E.

Army Form C. 2118.

Place	Date	Hour	Summary of Events and Information	Remarks and references to Appendices
FRESTIN X 28 b 5-9 FRANCE	1st	09:30	Parade for work in Camp. the 1st demobilized for Sommenn Erust Camp, 1st to U.K. 14 days leave.	
			6r 155 Field Coy. taken over Company funding Army HUGHES return from leave. Capt. H.E. Mc Keen proceed to U.K. by Boulogne draft SUMMAN, for repatriation to CANADA	
"	2nd	09:30	Parade for work in Camp. 1.O.R. 14 days leave U.K. 1.O.R. taken on strength from M.O.R.E.	
	3rd	09:30	Parade as above.	
	4th	10:00	Parade for checking 1.O.R. 14 days leave U.K. 1 O.R. reported from leave	
	5th	09:30	Parade for work in camp 1.O.R. 14 days leave O.R. + 1 O.R. reported from leave	
	6th	09:30	Parade as above. 1.O.R. 14 days leave U.K.	
	7th	09:30	Parade as above 1.O.R. 14 days leave U.K.	
	8th	09:30	Parade as above 1.O.R. 14 days leave U.K. + 2 O.R. despatched for demob.	
	9th	09:30	Parade as above 1.O.R. 14 days leave U.K.	
	10th	09:30	Parade as above 1.O.R. 14 days leave U.K. + 2 O.R. despatched for demob	
	11th	10:00	Parade for clothing 1.O.R. 14 days leave U.K.	
	12th	09:30	Parade for work in camp. 1.O.R. 14 days leave U.K. + 1 O.R. despatched for demob Driver BOCK. A.J. appointed Lance Cpl.	
	13th	09:30	Parade as above. 1.O.R. 14 days leave U.K.	
	14th	09:30	Parade as above 1.O.R. 14 days leave U.K. = 1 O.R. reported from leave	
	15th	09:30	Parade as above 1.O.R. 14 days leave U.K.	

Army Form C. 2118.

CADRE

156 Field Coy R.E.

Instructions regarding War Diaries and Intelligence
Summaries are contained in F. S. Regs., Part II.
and the Staff Manual respectively. Title pages
will be prepared in manuscript.

WAR DIARY

INTELLIGENCE-SUMMARY.

(Erase heading not required.)

Page II

Ref LH 36 75/6000
MAY 1919
FRANCE

Place	Date	Hour	Summary of Events and Information	Remarks and references to Appendices
FRETIN. X.26.b.5.9.	16th	09.30	Parade for work in Camp. 2 O.R. 14 days leave U.K.	AR
	17th	09.30	Parade as above. 2 O.R. 14 days leave U.K. 1 O.R. rejoined from leave. Major A.E. HUGHES. R.E. rejoined from leave to O.K.	AR
	18th	10.00	Parade for checking. 1 O.R. admitted hospital.	AR AR
	19th	09.30	Parade for work in camp. 2 O.R. 14 days leave U.K. - 1 O.R. rejoined from leave.	AR
	20th	09.30	Parade as above. 3 O.R. 14 days leave. O.K. - 1 O.R. rejoined from leave. Guard withdrawn from LILY DUMP - TEMPLEUVE.	AR
	21st	09.30	Parade as above. 1 O.R. 14 days leave U.K.	AR
	22nd	09.30	Parade as above. 1 O.R. 14 days leave U.K. 2 O.R. rejoined from leave. Major A.E. HUGHES. R.E. despatched for demobilisation. Major H. HOLBROW. R.E. takes over command 155 + 156 Coys, and 2nd Lt. T.S. BOWES. R.E. to supervise 156 Coy.	AR AR
	23rd	09.30	Parade as above. 2 O.R. 14 days leave U.K. 1 O.R. rejoined from leave.	AR
	24th	09.30	Parade as above. 1 O.R. rejoined from leave.	AR
	25th	10.00	Parade for checking. 1 O.R. rejoined from leave.	AR
	26th	09.30	Parade for work in Camp.	AR
	27th	09.30	Parade as above. 1 O.R. 14 days leave. U.K.	AR

Army Form C. 2118.

CADRE 156 Field Coy. R.E.

WAR DIARY
or
INTELLIGENCE SUMMARY.   Page III

(Erase heading not required.)

Ref. Sh. 36. 40000   FRANCE   MAY 1919.

Place	Date	Hour	Summary of Events and Information	Remarks and references to Appendices
FRETIN	2nd	09.30	Parade for work in Camp. 2 O.R. 14 days leave U.K. – 1 O.R. rejoined fr. leave	
	29th	09.30	Parade as above. 2 O.R. 14 days leave U.K. – 1 O.R. rejoined fr. leave	
X28b.5.9	30th	09.30	Parade as above. 1 O.R. 14 days leave U.K. – 1 O.R. rejoined fr. leave	
	31st	09.30	Parade as above. 1 O.R. 14 days leave U.K. – 1 O.R. rejoined fr. leave	

N Wollum Major RE
O.C. 156th Field Co., R.E.

www.ingramcontent.com/pod-product-compliance
Lightning Source LLC
Chambersburg PA
CBHW081407160426
43193CB00013B/2121